On Bitches

A Caveman's Treatise: Why Women Are Screwed Up and How Men May Deal with Them

Men, Your Flight Has Landed. Welcome to Planet Bitchstorm!

In order to retain your testicles and preserve your masculine psychology, you will be relegated to living in a metaphoric cave—and if the bitch you married permits, perhaps an actual man cave in the basement of HER house.

Before offloading, be certain to take a copy of **On Bitches** with you. It is located next to the oxygen mask in the emergency panel above your seat. Do not take the stairs. Those are for your stewardess. After her departure, hit the testosterone switch above you—the blue one if you watched her leave, the pink one if you were combing your hair.

When you splash down, swim—without breathing or swallowing—toward the towering obelisk that penetrates the bitch sky to you left. If you hit the pink button, or take in any of the liquid, just keep swallowing and drown. It's the estrogen pond, men, your first of many tests!

A Punch Buggy Book, in association with "On Your Knees" Publishing and "Take the Load" editing, located in the Bat Cave east of Space Mountain

With contributions by Lili Hun, the Bitch Smiter

Contributions by Genghis Khan, with James LaFond

Books by James LaFond

Nonfiction

The Fighting Edge, 2000
The Logic of Steel, 2001
The First Boxers, 2011
The Gods of Boxing, 2011
All Power Fighting, 2011
When You're Food, 2011
The Lesser Angles of Our Nature, 2012
The Logic of Force, 2012
The Greatest Boxer, 2012
Take Me to Your Breeder, 2014
The Streets Have Eyes, 2014
Panhandler Nation, 2014
The Ghetto Grocer, 2014
American Fist, 2014
Don't Get Boned, 2014
Alienation Nation, 2014
In The Chinks of The Machine, 2014
How the Ghetto Got My Soul, 2014
Saving the World Sucks, 2014
Taboo You, 2014
Winter of a Fighting Life, 2014
Narco Night Train, 2014

Into the Mountains of Madness: in [3 volumes], 2014
Incubus of Your Sacred Emasculation, 2014
Breeder's Digest, 2014
The Third Eye, 2015
Modern Agonistics, 2015
By the Wine Dark Sea, 2015
The Pale Usher, 2016
The End of Masculine Time, 2015
War Drums, 2015
A Thousand Years in His Soul: The Poets, 2015
A Thousand Years in His Soul: The Seers, 2015
Of Lions and Men, 2015
Your Trojan Whorse, 2016
On Bitches, 2016
Equidistant Drowning Babies, 2015
The Boned Zone, 2015
A Sickness of the Heart: Part One, 2015
Let the Weak Fall, 2015
If I Were King, 2015
Dark Art of an Aryan Mystic, 2015
Welcome to Harm City: White Boy, 2015
When You're Food: Raw, 2016
The Punishing Art, 2016
Twerps, Goons and Meatshields, 2016
Our Captain, 2016

Stillbirth of A Nation, 2016
America in Chains, 2106
40,000 Years from Home, 2016
The Sardonyx Stone, 2017
Neanderthal Resistance, 2016
Habitat Hoodrat: Ho Nation, 2016
When Your Job Sucks, 2016
A Once Great Medieval City, 2016
Right on White Time, 2016
A Well of Heroes: One, 2016
A Well of Heroes: Two, 2016
Paleface Sunset, 2016
Thriving in Bad Places, 2016
Into Wicked Company, 2016
Dawn in Dindustan, 2016
When Your Job Sucks, 2016
Good Morning, Dindustan! 2016
Habitat Hoodrat: Yo Nation, 2016
The Combat Space, 2017
A Dread Grace: One, 2017
The Liver-Eater Reader, 2017
Lunch at Café Dindustan, 2017
In Words, 2017
Slave Nation, 2017
Why Grownups Suck, 2017
A Dread Grace: Two, 2017

A Well of Heroes: Three, 2017
The Boxer Dread, 2017

Fiction
Astride the Chariot of Night, 2014
Sacrifix, 2014
Rise, 2014
Motherworld, 2014
Planet Buzzkill, 2014
Fruit of The Deceiver, 2014
Forty Hands of Night, 2014
Black and Pale, 2014
Daughters of Moros, 2014
Darkly, 2014
This Design is Called Paisley, 2015
Hurt Stoker, 2015
Poet, 2016
Triumph, 2015
Winter, 2015
The Spiral Case, 2016
Hemavore, with S. L. James, 2016
Yusuf of the Dusk, 2016
Beyond the Pale, 2017
RetroGenesis: Day 1, with Erique Watson, 2015
Easy Chair, 2015

Happily Ever Under, 2015
Road Killing, 2015
Fat Girl Dancing, 2015
Buzz Bunny, 2015
T. Spoone Slickens, Inquire, 2015
Dream Flower, 2015
The Song of Jeannot, 2015
Organa, 2015
A Hoodrat Halloween, 2015
Buzz Bunny, 2015
The Consultant, 2015
Reverent Chandler, 2015
He, 2016
Little Feet Going Nowhere, 2016
DoomFawn, 2016
The Jericho Bone, 2016
Ire and Ice, 2016
Night City, 2016
Night Song of the Nords, 2016
The Absolvant, 2017
Kettle of Bones, 2017
Wendigo, 2017
Sold, 2017

Sunset Saga Novels

Big Water Blood Song, 2011
Ghosts of the Sunset World, 2011
Beyond the Ember Star, 2012
Comes the Six Winter Night, 2012
Thunder-Boy, 2012
The World is Our Widow, 2013
Behind the Sunset Veil, 2013
Den of The Ender, 2013
God's Picture Maker, 2014
Out of Time, 2015
Seven Moons Deep, 2016
WhiteSkyCanoe, 2017

This book is dedicated Andrew Dice Clay, poet of Ancient Amurika:

"Hickory, dickory dock,

Why don't you..."

And Doctor Daniel London, who began this book and left its completion to me as he kayaked up the Amazon River in search of a fabled plant, the leaf of which exudes and estrogen blocking compound...

Table of Contents

Prologue

Taffy and Tiffany
Columbine Joe, On Bitches

Brother, I'm three wives deep now, and the oldest daughter, from the first—who was raised to believe I was a total bad guy, but who found out that I looked her up, so I could pay her child support after her mother skipped town with her—she wants to know what I looked like when I was Nineteen—in full Columbine Joe mode. Funny thing is, the only picture I could find was this prom picture with Taffy, who had actually asked Tiffany permission to have me escort her to the prom. And it was what it was supposed to be—a platonic date. However, they both knew I had been with the other—and as it turned out, I would be again.

Now Taffy had the kind of body—as you can see—that you want to have fun with. Her mother must have had a visitation from the Angel of the Lord telling her that her unborn child was destined to be a stripper, because she was. Why else would a woman saddle her girl with the ultimate white trash name? I was all over that, so much so that I would have thought she was pregnant with my child, had the kid not come out looking like Dwayne "The Rock" Johnson. Didn't need a DNA test for that—that boy had far too good a tan to be an Irishman.

Once, they both ended up at my place at the same time. I'm trying to maintain control by using separate kitchen chairs for each of us so that one doesn't start getting cuddly with me in front of the other. My roommate shows up and he's like, "Dude, why are both of your girls here at the same time?" and I'm like, "Could you keep it down, please. This is a miscalculation, a momentary lapse of knowing where the fuck my dick is supposed to be tonight, okay!"

Eventually Taffy leaves, claiming that I was ignoring her, which I of course copped to later on. She was also terrified of Tiffany. Tiffany is your Rhonda Rousey-type, corn-fed, Herford girl. I used to grapple with her all the time. And she'd love it, punch and kick me, head butt my chest. She wouldn't quit until I choked her out. My friends even broke it up once thinking that I was seriously abusing her and I'm like, "No man, she loves this shit."

Now, she couldn't take a guy, but any normal chick, oh it would be like a pit bull on a poodle. As it turns out I did not marry Taffy, which was a good thing. She turned out to be a terrible mother. She used to lock her kid in his room while she went to work. I'm not the guy that would be okay with my son getting locked in a fucking closet while my Ex was working the stripper pole. No wonder these people are so messed up today. Tiffany is a done deal too, but that was half my fault. I got a chance to hook back up with her lately—she really has her act together, halfway through medical school—but God himself cock-blocked me. She was number 2, all time, right behind the insane black chick whose middle name was drama—you don't answer the phone by the third ring and she's throwing shit at you when you get home. There is just something about extremely sexy women that—well, they're insane, that's it, isn't it?

Do you know of anyone that is hiring fulltime?

As a principled libertarian—unlike the gun-grabber my party nominated—I can't do Obama care and am doing without insurance. I eat well—am a personal trainer, doing the paleo-diet. But no one will hire you fulltime anymore because they don't want to have to provide health care. Obama is such a dick. He's made us into a nation of part-time employees. I've got eighty bucks after child support. If it wasn't for working at the liquor store and the personal training gig, I'd be living in the woods.

I am interested in dating again since the wife put me out and filed—and I was totally on the straight and narrow, doing my ministry on facebook, witnessing. But here I am, cast out and taxed for my rejection. As a Libertarian, I advocate dealing with women the same way I deal with cops, which I learned back when I was getting high all the time.

If a cop asks me what I'm doing, I say, "My business."

If he asks where am I going? I say, "To my business. Am I being detained, officer? Then have a nice day."

Once I had a few friends over to drink and smoke some weed, back around Two-Thousand. A knock comes on the door, and since they all knock the same, you know it's the police. I go up to the door and say, "May I help you"—speaking through the door. Mind you, I'm toking on a big old blunt. And my friends are flipping the fuck out."

The cop then says, "We have a noise complaint."

I stepped away, turned the music down, and said, "Is that an acceptable volume, officer?"

He said it was and then asked if he could enter, to which I said, "No sir, the noise complaint has been addressed. I won't turn it back up. Now have a nice day."

I went back to the couch and my friends are like, "You can do that?"

I said, "Absolutely, brother. They have a rule book and it behooves us to read it."

Introduction

Permit me to title the chapters that should have constituted my contribution to this misogynistic cause, but were not included—and I'm blaming it on the Lonely Man in the Boat. :

The Lonely Man in the Boat

Drowning the Lonely Man in the Boat

Throwing the Lonely Man in the Boat to the Sharks

Rescuing the Lonely Man in the Boat

Enslaving the Lonely Man in the Boat

It is obvious that my theory is that our women are currently oppressed by penis envy and must be returned to their natural place, which is a problem, being that I can only accommodate one of them at a time!

Summary

The Caveman's Treatise is a rational investigation into the completely fucked up mind and psyche of the modern day female. From the dawn of time to present day it is intolerantly clear to all men that women are full of shit. They have no idea what they want, how they want it and to what degree. When they get what they want, they get rid of it, yet continuing to bemoan their plight in selected despair at the expense of a man's gracious protection, love and fulfillment. The Cavemen dissect the insanity that permeates the female cortex in irrational and deceptive neurologic dysfunction, to the dismay of men everywhere. All men will cherish this text. Women will hate it, well..........because they are women and they hate everything, unless they actually love it; but that might mean they actually have to make a fucking decision on the IT, whatever they decide the IT is!

Feeding The Bitch

Three Mistakes That Beg to be Made on the Married Man's Path to After-Marital Hell

He just stared in wonderment and confusion. What started as a simple discussion two years ago ended with him saying goodbye to the kids and signing over the home of 24 years to his now ex-wife. Just like that, so it seemed, his life was turning and it was the wrong turn on the wrong street.

All she said was, "Why do you love me."

He thought, for what seemed like a life time for her, but in reality was only a microsecond.

WHY, because I do. Or so he thought. And so he stated.

"I could give you a hundred reasons, but I just do. You are everything to me."

He clearly thought that would do it, but the confused mind of a fragile female is never something to take for granted in any form. Her form was morphing into the creature he was always warned about, but never knew or accepted as fact. The animal hybrid of destructive demise was thundering her roar and jostling for a battle.

"NO! I want to know; why do you love me?"

Again he thought, but responded from his heart. "I love you for hundreds of reasons, and I love you for no reason at all. I just LOVE YOU."

With that, he inquired as to the development of this line of questioning, which of course was Mistake Number Two.

Mistake Number One was even thinking he could rationalize a thought or feeling with someone who only existed on thought or feeling. Rationalization requires objective insight. Objectivity does not exist in the future fighting female intent on destructive discussion and debilitating discourse.

Jack loved his wife of 24 years. He thought she loved him. But day after day since the primordial scream of insanity began with an unanswerable question, Jack found Jill incessantly irrational.

"Your answer is not enough. I need concrete reasons." That was her daily inquiry.

Trying to rationalize this insanity further, Jack listed reason after reason, from the way she smiled to the way she touched him. How she moaned during animal sex, or coyly purred during cuddling time, something Jack despised but did because he knew it made her happy. And, of course, he enjoyed making his wife happy because that's what *A GOOD FUCKING HUSBAND DOES!*

100-plus reasons later and still Jill could not wrap her hands around the concept of his love for her. Just like she couldn't wrap her hand around his manhood like they used to twice per day. Yeah, that stopped to.

24 years of six days a week work. Taking on the second job so she could go to school and earn a degree. Staying up late with the kids so she could sleep for the next day's exam. Disgusting dinners of inedible food because the BITCH never did learn how to cook like his mom. But he stayed and continued to love her. Take out the trash, fix the plumbing, clean the bathroom and garage, make the money, pay the bills. She could stay home and do whatever the FUCK she wanted and he was fine with that. Just feed him, fuck him once in a while and be his friend. Sound familiar. IT SHOULD! It is a simple recurring theme. He didn't need much or even want much. Yet she needed and wanted everything. So she got it. Because that what a good husband does... gives his wife the best of everything at his own sacrifice.

IT wasn't enough. IT became something else, some other need not yet met, and the monster grew, evolved into a creature of despair and inquisitive stupidity with questions like "WHY DO YOU LOVE ME?"

So he asked back in return, "Well, baby... Why do you love me?"

The answer...no there wasn't any. Not even a burp, fart or even groan. She just walked away in disgust huffing and puffing.

"Don't turn this around on me."

Mistake Number Three: Thinking there could actually be a mutual discussion on any topic. Mutual requires and implies willingness. When the woman is not willing, the man is found to hand satisfaction in the basement at his own sexual demise. When the woman is not willing, "FINE" means that everything is wrong, but nothing will be discussed because I AM NOT WILLING! When the woman is not willing, sex becomes a chore as does making a simple sandwich after a long day of work. When the woman is not willing, justification becomes action and action becomes justified. Women do that well. Anything, action or thought can then be justified. WHY DO YOU LOVE ME now has to be justified. Even though it had been for 24 years.

Jill started all the nonsense over a simple question. What initiated that thought in the frontal cortex of the female creature will never be known or understood. Jack thought his answer to be appropriate because it was true and sincere and from the heart. But, unknowingly, it was not an answerable question. Now his heart was screaming as he watched the kids drive away, and he had his own questions.

From one question spurred argument after argument, counseling sessions, weekly, and family discussions. The counseling sessions continued because the counselor continually sided with Jack but Jill could not have that so let's beat the proverbial dead penis until someone, anyone agrees with Jill.

But no one did, agree with Jill that is. Jack was left to beat his own penis. So, of course she was right, and everyone including enemy #1 (the husband) was wrong. The monster gorged on irrational emotion. Emotion became motion and she emotionally meandered her way out of the marriage, only to seek answers to a question she could not answer on her own.

"WHY DO YOU LOVE ME?"

BECAUSE I JUST DO....and that should be enough for any woman.

Somewhere Jill went off the deep end, nucking futs; or so Jack thought. But later he realized that was not the case. She was always crazy, he just didn't see it. BECAUSE HE WAS FUCKING IN LOVE WITH THE BITCH!

» Add a comment «

Ishmael   August 17, 2015 11:50 AM EDT

James, major cause of male insanity, to men that love women. Thank you James Ishmael.

Kman   August 16, 2015 12:29 PM EDT

VERY red pill!

The Friend Zone

Toying with The Toxic Compound, Estrogen

NO, men and women cannot be friends. Well, at least in the sense that men are friends with men, or women with women...if that can be called a friendship. Men being friends with other men, now that is a unique relationship of honor, and a bond reflected in being able to beat the shit out of one another and then forget why you were angry with one another and go have a drink fondly recalling yesteryear.

Men forgive and forget.

Women do not forgive and never forget.

Women harbor hate, spite, and anger. They thrive on it. This is of course a product of the toxic compound, Estrogen. It is a danger to all mankind, and one day, medical science will find a cure for estrogen toxicity. Women are ruled by estrogen, and some other chemical delights.

Thus, a woman's inability to harbor these emotions is tied to their hormonal homeostasis. Just like their internal physiologic design, it doesn't forget; nor do they. Holy shit, they can remember what color your pants were on the first date and what day and time it was. Men can't remember yesterday. Simple, direct and honestly stated.

The cavemen know that the male psyche evolved (or devolved depending on perspective) a possessive gene which doesn't not allow platonic existence. We fake it, because ultimately if the bitch be hot we be on the prowl.

But women will disagree about being friends. They are wrong, as usual. But we will let them disagree because we want to be good "friends" that is. Even though we know we are not.

There, it is said.

So it is written, let it be done.

Now, off with their heads.

Hell, let's be realistic, women can't be friends with their own sex. Vindictive bitches can transform from that cute little snow flower to a dragon demon capable of eating their young. So how in Casanova's name can women be friends with men? Well, to clarify: women can think they can be friends with men, but men know they are just playing the game of friendship. So it is not mutual. And yes it is a game, perhaps not by intention or from ill will, but it is a façade, a show, a masquerade. Men have no choice. So in justification, their "façade" is even unintentional. Their little head will always think for the bigger head and the little head is more powerful, by any metric. Ultimately the little head will win. It always does.

From the splurge of testosterone explosion till death, men think of sex. Sex with women, unless they are gay, but that is not a topic of discussion because even gay men still think about sex. Women think about it too. They just like to fake the moral high ground by repressing their urges. Men live their urges every second of every day. Like a wise man once said, "Women need a reason for sex, Men just need a place." And that place can be with their "friend" if their "friend" decides not to be a friend anymore and be a "place."

Estrogen beasts, if your guy friend tells you that you are just friends, believe it. But also know that any given second, if you are vaguely hot, he will nail you. As a matter of fact, this could be the icing on the cake with the proverbial "friends with benefits" moniker in play.

Of course, this too is just plain bullshit. Men will be friends as long as it takes to "not be friends" and they nail you. Then they can go back to acting like your friend until the woman decides she wants to stop being friends long enough to release some of that estrogen toxicity in a session of unbridled head-banging, rumpus-bumping, and beddy bye pelvic grinding.

Whether you are a Caveman or an Estrogen Beast, enter The Friend Zone at your peril.

» Add a comment «
Ben Rumson August 17, 2015 11:20 PM EDT

ha,ha,ha,ha,ha,ha. Damn you're spot on! I love looking at women's "girls" that are tagged on their chests. I guess that's just wrong, but I always say, "It's OK to look at the menu as long as you come home for supper." Then I get bitch slapped...just because she can....because I did.

Peace out!

'Regular Bitches Still Call'

About Daniel "Cougar Killer" London, Author of On Bitches

Daniel London is a retired man of the town. A former escort and male prostitute, Daniel began his career as a physiologist in graduate school to advance to medical school. He was born in the Midwest to an Episcopalian minister and a meter maid mother who was notorious for forgiving tickets in return for sexual favors. He left the family early at 17. Poor and destitute, he fortuitously came upon a number of male escorts and prostitutes and thus learned his trade.

Three years of medical school solidified his knowledge of human anatomy and physiology, which he utilized in ongoing escort services that paid for medical school. In his third year his sexual prowess became well known among the cougar circuit. Income was exceptional, such that Daniel reconsidered his career path. Daniel left medical school the middle of his third year to concentrate full time on man whoring. His travels continued to the east coast New York, Philadelphia, and ending in Baltimore where he retired and lives comfortably off of stock investments and writing x rated novels and slutty smut books for horny bitches.

Daniel's dream was once again realized when he returned to chiropractic medical school achieving his Doctor of Chiropractic in 2014, only to have it stolen from him. In the midst of opening the Mondawmin Chiropractic Institute, the Baltimore Riots of 2015 burned his building to the ground before the sign could even be raised. For a brief time Daniel returned to man whoring in depression and depravity over the loss of his business. Daniel's first love would always be there and regular bitches still call on him today even in "retirement." It was during his sojourn from the trade that "On Bitches" was realized. With long-time friend, confidant and wingman, James LaFond—who used to watch the "Cougar Killer's" Mercedes on those demanding occasions when Queeneequa [the author's fat black female pimp] scheduled Daniel for dalliances across the color line—Daniel took to writing the definitive treatise on the woman's psyche.

Meatheads and Mother Bears

Nesting and Its Implications for Your Man Cave by Lili Hun

In consideration of a few things I've read here, which always lead me down the path of differences between men and women, I'd like to explore nesting as an activity which can get the better of both mating partners.

Reading from this site has increased my curiosity about our male / female differences. Usually, a concept from an article stays with me, periodically swimming to the surface of my awareness, treading water, while I consider its appearance in my mind.

I've noticed that when I open this web page, the pull-down box of titles you can view on the site (within the Contents block on the right side of the page) varies willy-nilly, like the entertaining Magic 8 Ball from my childhood. This morning, synchronistically enough, considering my subject, I noticed the enticing title, On Bitches, and smiled—-surely a sign that I was exploring in the right direction.

So I quote from the venerable author of this site, in Happily Ever Under: Chapter 4, Under The Paleface, Materialism RedJacket And JillSong Shooting Bull (whose picture will also randomly greet me in the Featured Titles block, elegantly framed, bloody nose dripping copiously and obscuring the handsome features of the author, or at least making him difficult to look at...).

"Our goods? Woman, if you appeal to my father for a divorce and he grants it, you keep it all, and all I have is Swift Knife and my weapons. It is your stuff—all of your fancy paleface junk—so you haul it."

My lines of inquiry were, of course, based on broad gender strokes, because there are men whose garages and homes are overflowing with their own rainy-day-useful goods as well (and downsizing and organization is a common subject these days):

1. How is nesting defined, in both the animal and human world?

2. What is the life cycle of nesting?

3. Who guards the nest?

4. If nesting in our human world is represented by the accumulation of goods that ensure the survival of those in it, is hoarding nesting gone bad?

5. Is there a socioeconomic precedent for hoarding (remember the stories of older relatives who had survived the great depression and saved pieces of string, etc.); or is it just symptomatic of materialism, isolation from a helping tribe, a rank mental disorder?

6. Is nesting also marking territory?

7. What is the connection between women and materialism, manifested in nesting and why?

8. Is cleaning while emotionally upset another form of nesting, and how does it serve?

9. Nesting and sex?

10. Is there a way to work with this gender culture clash that is not extreme in its approach?

11. And last but not least, what is this land of bitches, and how does a woman or man know when she's not in Kansas anymore?

The Land of Bitches is the realm of people [male, female or mangina] that a man may not beat, throttle or otherwise harm, without compromising his sense of honor—so is somewhat subjective. [JL]

Selected Definitions of Nesting

1. Most commonly an avian formation or protected place to lay eggs and rear young, though other species have these as well.

2. The negative of this, as in "a nest of vice."

3. To fit together or within each other.

4. To settle or place something in or as if in a nest.

5. In computing, the enclosure of one block of code inside another.

For a complete list of definitions, please see links referenced.

Selected Synonyms of Nest (chosen for their use by and related to men)

Den, refuge, hideaway, lair, roost, haunt, lodge, retreat, sanctuary, cave, lodge, quarters, shelter, and within this category, a base of operations.

A Few Random Expressions

1. Den of iniquity
2. To rule the roost
3. Thieves hideaway
4. Dragon's lair

Life Cycle of Nesting

This is often described as an activity the female engages in shortly before the arrival of her young. It may involve cleaning, organizing, uncharacteristic bursts of energy to accomplish these, obsessive (or not) attention to preparing, protecting and controlling the environment for the safety and comfort of those within it, including the screening of those who are trustworthy enough to merit entry therein.

Relative to the life cycle of nesting, I don't see these behaviors as limited to impending maternity, nor even to females, reflected in parts of the animal world and my chosen synonyms list. I also see the degree to which we engage in these activities as something affected by personality, not just gender or life stage.

As for who guards the nest, it may be guarded by both male and female or sat in by the female while guarded by the male. So much of the time, the nest is important to both.

Hoarding occurs in parts of the animal world, relative to keeping a food supply for survival. In the human world, the same may apply with a wider range of things hoarded for survival and is affected by anticipation or actuality of a large-scale disaster event. And yes, it would seem that when you can no longer move safely within your nest nor find what you need to function effectively or survive, due to extreme accumulation, there is something abnormal, running counter to survival, involved. Enough said on hoarding, I think.

Regarding the socioeconomic precedent involved, one expression comes to mind: the haves and the havenots. This great divide is exacerbated in our culture by materialism, capitalism, ideology, cultural hegemony expressed via the media, breakdown of the tribe and the family (particularly the extended family and family isolated by great distance from its extensions), the American idealization of personal independence and pathologizing of those with limited tolerance for living in isolation (actually runs totally counter to our survival instincts and behaviors), as well as other things I haven't thought of. It just doesn't seem logical that the list of influences would be so short. You're welcome to contribute here.

Beaver—no pun intended—seem to be the ultimate nesting creatures, and they were tragically easy to kill by tool-using predators, due to their resulting fixed locations. [JL]

And of course, there are rank mental disorders in abundance in our culture. Our inability to toe the many dysfunctional lines described above results in varying dysfunctional coping mechanisms as well as simply going crazy in response to the tortures, mental and otherwise, inflicted by our society. If in doubt consider NAMI stats on this (referenced). Oddly enough, the CDC rates reported are much lower, which in my mind may be explained by who is collecting the data, their agenda for its use, and motivation to report accurately based on personal factors like work ethic of the employees and politics of the collecting institution. Also note that suicide rates vary by state, gender, race, and age; surviving a suicide may skew the rates also.

Moving on, is nesting also marking territory? In brief, it seems to fit.

In terms of women and materialism, the most obvious connection would be our society's materialism, conditioning all to get on the wage slave treadmill, increasing the speed of acquisition ability, until you ultimately fall off, falling from the social perch that your acquisitions allowed you to tentatively balance on. The more this is socially emphasized, the more uninquiring minds want the loot, particularly women who have needed to ensure their own safety and the safety of their young via their mate's ability to line the nest. This seems to be an ancient concern exacerbated by modern creation of artificial material needs where there were none. This somehow reminds me of a fairy tale of the fish with the three wishes and the greedy wife.

The only connection that can be drawn between cleaning when upset and nesting, is the fact that cleaning is a part of nesting. I suppose when we are disturbed by something we cannot control, it can provide a small measure of comfort to cozy up our own nest.

Based on the definitions of nesting I've read, I've decided that sex is nesting physically with one another, and that kind of nesting begets another kind of nesting which this article has been dedicated to exploring. There's a hormonal connection here. Women are loaded with oxytocin near the end of pregnancy and postpartum, when they will be nesting and soon bonding.

During sex, dopamine floods our brains, much like any other addicting drug, activating our "feel good center" of the brain.

Oxytocin gets released too, same bonding chemical ensuring mother/baby bonding. And the surprise: serotonin levels drop so that we get a little more anxious and less complacent about keeping up with the person we just mated with. Evidently if they stayed high, we wouldn't be concerned with who we just mated with, we'd just go on and mate with the next one.

So nature pretty much ensures that we get screwed after screwing, particularly when we haven't adequately vetted the object of our desire, leading to overstayed entanglements, commonly occurring sometime or other with all of us...

How would I try to work with the gender culture clash without being extreme?

Hmmm. Dunno. Let me try wrapping up my thoughts.

As seen by words for male nests, as well in certain subjects expounded upon on previously on this site, the lair or roost is of equal importance to the nest and treatment of it is often a source of conflict leading to banishment of one party from it by the other. There's no foolproof formula for ensuring that your lair or nest remains as you want it to with an additional occupant of any relation to you.

With intimate partners of any nature or degree, truly take a good length of time to get to know your mate before sharing: know their personality, characteristics, strengths, defects, patterns of behavior (particularly under stress), and how this blends within that person and mixes with your own mental and emotional brew.

Observe, more than talk about, their value system, as it appears in the overall pattern of their life: actions, habits, behaviors, etc. Evidently, there is no greater marker for success, however you may partner up (in business, friendship, etc.) than shared values.

If you want to give that bitch a fair shake, and I use this term most affectionately in the breeding sense, with or without cohabitation, base your considerations on what's really in front of you, not on what happened with the last 10 bitches, without dispensing with your good sense and maintaining a balanced perspective. We all have some ugly defects, so what can you live with?

I have also found certain time markers to be fairly critical. Generally, people can't keep their masks on forever. Three months is often when the real person starts to show up. If you make it to the two / three year line, you have been able to amass significant amounts of information. Don't whitewash it. You may discover a sociopath at any point unless they are gifted at staying in disguise or you were so desperate for that particular female apparition that you never read her accurately at any point along the way and always seem to fall for the same type (see the Hot-Crazy Matrix referenced by other readers for help with this).

http://www.bing.com/videos/search?q=the+hot+crazy+matrix+james+yeager&FORM=VIRE1#view=detail&mid=A01469FFB650E17D312FA01469FFB650E17D312F

As for women knowing when they themselves have stomped off to or been banished to the land of bitches, this can be tricky. For one thing, it requires a woman's awareness of her own patterns of relating and defects. If she's always pointing the finger at someone else, let her be. If, as the woman, you like this meathead quite a bit, and the feeling is mutual, and you realize that you have just bitten, or he behaves as if you have bitten, immediately apologize for a mistaken strike based on your own short comings or for an unintended wound.

As for being sent there due to a misunderstanding or a shortcoming of his, know that you're not in control of, nor understand, what churns about in the minds of men. You will not be banished there forever, nor will he stay growling dire warnings from it and ignoring you forever. Cultivate your interests. You both need a life if you are to share from it.

Lili Hun

Thank you, Lili.

Links

https://en.wiktionary.org/wiki/nesting

http://dictionary.reference.com/browse/nesting

http://www.thesaurus.com/browse/nesting

http://www.dailymail.co.uk/sciencetech/article-2423557/Why-pregnant-women-obsessed-tidying-nesting-Its-inner-cavewoman.html

http://www.wm.edu/news/stories/2012/among-the-eagles-deadbeat-dads,-nest-intrusions-and-cheating-wives123.php

https://en.wikipedia.org/wiki/Nest

http://www.factmonster.com/ipka/A0768562.html

https://en.wikipedia.org/wiki/Hoarding

nami.org/factsheets/mentalillness_factsheet.pdf

http://psychcentral.com/news/2011/10/25/antidepressant-use-up-400-percent-in-us/30677.html

http://www.cdc.gov/nchs/data/databriefs/db76.htm

https://en.wikipedia.org/wiki/Gender_differences_in_suicide#United_States

http://www.cbsnews.com/pictures/suicide-20-states-with-highest-rates/

http://www.suicide.org/suicide-statistics.html

http://scholarshipupdates.org/tags/suicide-rates-in-the-united-states.html

http://pluripotentnurse.blogspot.com/2008/08/hormones-released-during-sexual.html

http://www.youramazingbrain.org/lovesex/sciencelove.htm

When to Walk Away from Her

An On Bitches Chapter published at Single Dude Travel.com

Manuel Pfister has published an original nonfiction piece of mine at Single Dude Travel.com. If you have read The Mac Daddy versus Big Shiv, recall that this is almost the identical crew. The mid portion of the article consists of Lord of the Lezbos, which is the first ghetto grocer tale I told about that crew, and serves as an effective introduction to the personalities involved.

Check it out at the link below.

http://www.singledudetravel.com/2015/09/archies-woe-a-cautionary-tale-of-young-lust-from-the-ghetto-grocer/

Archie's Woe, A Cautionary Tale of Young Lust from the Ghetto Grocer
by James LaFond · September 7, 2015

Author's Note

I am currently co-writing a book with Daniel London titled, On Bitches, most of which is being serialized online, before being assembled for print publication. Manuel Pfister at Single Dude Travel has expressed an interest in work place stories that might address the sexual specifics of being a Single Dude. So here it goes, a pained tale of young love to which I was an unwilling party, and which still haunts me 15 years on...

The Crew

Night crews in supermarkets—especially Baltimore City supermarkets—can be as chock full of characters as a Foreign Legion squad. I will introduce them by way of an old story that I have published in a book on writing that almost nobody will read.

Lord of the Lezbos or 'Harm City Island'

How Would Regular People Recreate Society?: A Creative Writing Exercise Gone Awry
© 2013 James LaFond

I have received e-mails and comments from readers—all far more intelligent than the people I normally associate with—concerning the questions of masculinity, feminism and society. A decade or so back I did a creative writing experiment that sheds some light on how the normal person thinks.

What us writers and avid readers often forget is that almost nobody writes and very few people read beyond the level of advertisements and warnings. I have often used working class and criminal people as models for primitive characters in fiction.

[2014 insert] Ann Sterzinger, in her recent review, and in an e-mail, hinted that I am reluctant to succeed commercially as a writer as it would endanger my status as a laborer and cut off the source for much of my character information. I must admit that there is something to her theory. How would I write another ancient slave believably and at variance from previous depictions if not for the inspiration of the wage slaves I share my life with?

So, for those men and women who wonder what things might look like if we suddenly started from scratch again, here is one possibility.

Just before New Year's it is annually my habit to try and convert as many of my handwritten notes to computer files as possible. So, I thought it was about time to file away this faded memo pad from late December 1999. I do not know if you are old enough to recall, but it was supposed to be the end of the world as we knew it: Y2K. All computers would go into digital menopause and the world of finance, the power grid, the 'Star Wars' array, would all of a sudden be married to a raging virtual female of global girth.

Back then, I was winding up my research on the Violence Project, and preparing to dive headfirst into a huge ancient boxing project which entailed the reading of over 1,000 books. I wanted to take a break from the nonfiction grind and write something fun, but lacked the mental energy. My coworkers, on the inner city supermarket night crew, began discussing the End Times which were nigh. Since I was the only employee who could actually decipher the union handbook I was regarded as something of a Lex Luther type genius, and always consulted on such matters.

I decided on a self-serving writing exercise, once attempted by my 7th Grade teacher, until some 13 year-old psychopath ruined it. I thought this exercise might provide me with a storyline to go with the crazy characters I worked with. The concept was to ask a group of people what they would do if they were all of a sudden shipwrecked together on a desert island, with no foreseeable chance of rescue.

My method was to ask everyone three questions at break time [midnight] and then see them about their answers at lunchtime [3:00 a.m.]. In the meantime they would be alone in their work areas, and unable to share information. After setting the stage briefly, I asked them:

1. What would your immediate goal be?
2. What would be your first action?
3. What would be your second action if the first action went poorly?

Infantis Personae

My cast was quizzed from highest ranking to lowest [by position and seniority], and consisted of the characters named below, according to the nickname they were known on the crew:

1. 'The Dark Elf' or 'Asshole' was the night crew captain, aged 35, short, and weighing in at about 125 pounds. The Dark Elf was a lazy, rural, white back-stabber who took credit from and laid blame on the crew that did his work while he played nerf football or read the newspaper.

2. 'Buster' AKA 'The Forty-Year-Old Virgin,' was the loyal, dimwitted, second man, about 200 pounds of stubborn urban white resolve.

3. 'Silverback' was the senior clerk, a 60-year-old black man from the Deep South, who stood six-two and scaled about 260 ponds.

4. 'Bigboy,' was the frozen foods clerk, a black, 35-year-old former minor league football player and street thug from Washington D.C. [Bigboy and Silverback had previously engaged in a brawl in the lunchroom, resulting in a bite wound and a drawn razor.]

5. JoJo was the deli clerk, a hard-talking former street-fighter. Although she weighed in at only 105 pounds and was 45 years of age, this white chick was, pound-for-pound, regarded as the toughest person on the crew.

6. 'Archie' AKA 'Sissy Boy,' at six-foot and seven-inches tall, this 21-year-old white clerk was inclined to poetry and group sex.

7. Liz, at 25-years-old, was a curvy natural blonde cashier who pulled in about a half-dozen cops every night, eager to chat her up rather than fight crime.

8. 'Sammy,' a 20-year-old gay mixed race clerk, was the new guy on the crew, and was being targeted for economic death by 'The Dark Elf'.

9. 'Chiquito,' was an illegal Mexican immigrant who cleaned the floors at night. He scaled about 90 pounds, and was routinely tormented by Bigboy who he called 'El Gordo.'

Okay, so what could go wrong with this group of castaways? I only have their answers, having never written the story. I leave it to you, my readers, to come up with your own interpretation of the probable first 24-hours on Harm City Island. I was partially interested in how the existing hierarchy, such as it was, would hold up. I certainly wasn't expecting Gilligan's Island. The one thing that this crew had going for it over most crews, was that there were no alcoholics or drug addicts, which usually constitute 60% of a crew.

Goal-Action-Contingency, by Survivor

1. 'The Dark Elf': "Are you kidding me? I want to survive. That means I'll run my ass off for

the hills as soon as we hit the beach. Back-up plan? Run faster!"

2. 'Buster': "Kill The Dark Elf, strangle him most likely. If that doesn't work I'll drown him."

3. 'Silverback': "That Sweet Thang dare—gots ta have dat. First course will be to whoop dat Bigboy butt! Not kill him, jus' make an example—lay it down. If I lose? Hell, I guess I'd be stuck with JoJo—Oh hell no! Dat evil bitch like ta cut my throat in ma sleep. Shee, I guess I either take dat faggot or break in Sissy Boy—ya hea' dat Archie! You big sissy, you betta hope Bigboy don't whoop dis ass! Old fella might could use a hand! I'd have me a bitch one way o da otha."

4. 'Bigboy': "Liz. The rest a them fools be killin' the Boss. It a be a throw down with ole Silverback! He is a big boy—en bite like a goddamn rot. So, if I lose, I guess I'll settle fo JoJo."

5. 'JoJo': "Survive shit! Working this shitty job is survival. Living with a crazy drunk that beats my ass is survival. This would be my life's chance at a vacation! Okay, you know

Silverback and Bigboy will be fighting over Liz while the rest of those idiots kill The Boss. The loser will want me. No way. They are all ugly! I'd rather go lezzy with Liz. At least she's good looking. Whoever loses, Chiquito and me will kill in their sleep. Then, we go over and murder the other big bastard. Contingency shit. This works or I die trying. We will need men to work while I'm learning how to be a lezbo, and to fight in case cannibals show up. Buster and the sissy boys can live."

6. 'Archie': "The Dark Elf dies on the beach! That's it. Nothing else matters."

7. 'Liz': "Why would you ask the steak what its goals were just before you threw it to the dogs? I'll stick with JoJo and do what she says. I hope she doesn't pimp me out."

8. 'Sammy': "The men are all callous idiots. I will align myself with the women."

9. 'Chiquito': Our Vera Cruz native had very little English. He does draw a finger across the throat convincing though, as he did when he snarled, "El Gordo filete finito!" [Note: he was learning English, and his habit was to mix English and Spanish in the same sentence;

finito is Italian, not Spanish, so my guess is he was trying to say "finished" in regards to fileting the fatty.]

Conclusion

These folks did not describe all of the foraging and hut-building I would have expected. The surprising thing for me was the reliability with which they were able to predict each other's behavior. 6 of 9 individuals settled on violence as their first action. We had four basic choices uppermost, which were chosen at the following rates, from the top of the preexisting hierarchy to the bottom:

1. Survival: 1 in 9
2. Companionship: 2 in 9
3. Vengeance: 3 in 9
4. Alliance: 3 in 9

In retrospect, rather than as a story-generator, I like this as a crisis behavior predictor, as it was initially used by my poor school teacher. The vengeance results here would extrapolate to attacks on politicians in a fall of civilization scenario. It is also interesting that you immediately ended up with 2 blocks of weak and oppressed people [the entire bottom of the crew] who struck out at or allied themselves against those at the top of the existing hierarchy. Overall, violence clustered in the center of the existing hierarchy pyramid.

I don't know about you, but I think JoJo has a lock on the post-disaster power structure.

Archie's Woe

So there you have the crew that was present for the following story. Archie was an introspective former goth kid, who had been harassed in high school a lot after the Columbine shootings, being forcibly counseled by teachers, teased and picked on by jocks, and ignored by females in junior high school and high school. He was a towering broad-shoulder physical specimen with long Conan hair. He was, however, lacking in masculine character.

Once, while working the soda aisle, Big Boy talked Archie—who he used to slap around and wrestle into humiliating positions in the stockroom regularly—into threatening me over something trivial. Archie had recently transferred in from another store where he had worked with Big Boy, who was another recent acquisition. Archie did not know my reputation. Big Boy did, and grinned wryly as Archie stalked over to me, grabbed my long hair in his huge left hand, placed his box cutter to my throat, and then said that he was going to cut my hair.

I grabbed his penis and left nut, squeezed, twisted, and snarled something which I forget and he was soon submitting in a whining fashion. He came to me later and apologized. I made peace with him and offered to give him boxing lessons when he inquired about my level of twerp fearlessness, as these fellows towered over me like giants, but did not ever, insult or threaten me.

JoJo came to me, having heard about my heroics, and asked me how big Archie's dick was! I answered matter-of-factly, "He's well endowed. I could barely get my hand around the dick and the left nut."

She then gave me a twinkle of the eye—as she had had a crush on me for a couple of years after seeing me punk out a security guard—and skipped off in her animalistic, sexy, broken puppet kind of way.

After I made Archie grovel in the soda aisle Silverback and Big Boy would not let up, accusing him of being a "sissy' a "faggot" an "ass-licker" and "big ole bitch!"

Silverback rode him particularly hard, denying Archie's claims to be dating an attractive blonde, a senior in high school. Archie was, I think, 22, four years older than his girl. He showed us a picture of a tall blonde with elfin features, and still no one but I believed he was not gay or a virgin.

Archie's Girl

One night, on Archie's night off, he came into visit us with a fine looking girl—the girl in the photo—on his arm. He introduced her to JoJo and Liz, to me and Buster, and walked her by the night captain and the big black men disdainfully as Big Boy and the Dark Elf drooled. I thought they made a fine looking couple, with her standing a gracile six feet in sneakers next to his broad six-foot seven-inch frame.

After they left, JoJo skipped out in the aisle and said approvingly, "They are a cute couple."

As she skipped away, Silverback snorted, "Shee, dat notin' buta bag a bones—pretty do she may be. Ifin' a man gonna be large en in charge he needs himself some butt and some booby, some strong thigh—why, I jus assume lay pipe on dat drowned rat lookin' bitch JoJo."

Big Boy was more considered, "Shit nigga, she white ain't she? It's a brutha's duty ta smack dat snow booty!"

Silverback, as usual, dismissed Big Boy's opinion, "Is you blind, Fool? What booty—where?"

And on the insanity rolled.

Although everyone was polite around Archie's girl, when he came back to work only Buster, Sammy and Liz and I were complimentary and considered. The Dark Elf was talking about, "Gangbanging that jailbait," Silverback said, "Hey faggot, dough I don' normally lay pipe up on a white woman, if you girl need her some real lovin' send her on along, boy!"

The worst was Big Boy, who grabbed Archie by the arm, pressed him against the wall and snarled threats, such as, "You been holdin' out on me, Boy. I ought ta tax your ass for not passin' that pretty thing along to me—you know I got my needs, Archie!"

Archie was in a spot, being heckled all the more by his cruel coworkers. What was worse, we no longer had our own work areas, but "ganged" [sodomy metaphors abound in retail food] the store as one unit, working out ahead of Freddie, the Mexican floor tech, who scampered among these giant Americans like the ghost of some lost tribe.

Archie's Plea

Archie asked me to speak with him in the lunch room, which was a tiny space behind the scanning office and the two restrooms. He wanted to know if I found his girl attractive, and also how well-endowed I was. I stopped the line of inquiry with an admission that she was very pretty, but that, in my late thirties, I was not in the habit of thinking of women that age in a sexual light.

As we sat closely he confided in me, that although his love life with his elfin princess had been fulfilling, she wanted to experiment, she wanted a threesome. He had brought her in to work on his night off, not to show her off, but so that she could make a selection. He then dropped the bomb, "We want to have a threesome with you. I trust you and she finds you attractive."

I said, "Arch, she's fine enough, and I won't do it for two reasons: one, I have no desire to be naked in bed with your big ass. The other is, when I have sex with a woman, they fall in love with me—always. I don't know what I'm doing wrong. It's like a curse—I can't get rid of them."

Then, as he winced and began to gather his thoughts for a statement, the women's room door squeaked open and JoJo skipped out, over to us, threw her little butt up on the lunchroom table between us and said, "I think it's a great idea. I'll be the fluffer!"

"What the hell is a fluffer?" I asked, dumbfounded that the woman I had been taking to a motel room once a week behind our spouses backs, had been eavesdropping.

"It's the girl who blows all of the porno guys behind the scenes!"

I now felt like I was on the spot, and, recently learning how violent my little lady friend was, was now in a panic to find a way out of this situation, a way which did not smack of a rejection of her. Fortunately, Archie let me off the hook and made his life more miserable, with an ill-considered statement, "Get away you scary little woman—you are not invited!"

She immediately got angry—as was her temperament—and then scrunched her face in conspiratorial glee and skipped away, out into the aisle, to inform our savage little world. I patted him on the back and went to work, apologizing for not being able to oblige him and his lady.

The rest of the night was pure torment for Archie. Through it all he continued to plead with me, even in front of the other crew members, to have sex with his girlfriend, assuring me that he would not touch me, that he was not gay, and that she just wanted to experience being penetrated by two men at the same time.

Silverback was uproariously critical, laughing and joking all night, with such quips as, "Hey Big Boy, you hea da joke 'bout da two white boys en da light bulb? Hey, Big Boy, how many white boys do it take ta lay pipe on but one bitch?"

I could not fathom Archie's persistence. Finally, he said to me, almost in tears, "I have to get a second guy. She really needs to experience this and said if I couldn't arrange it that she would."

Finally, I said, "Man, I'm really sorry. It's bad enough that I'm cheating on my wife. But if you think I'm going to take a chance of cheating on JoJo, then come to work and turn my back on her while she's got a case cutter in her hand, you have another thing coming. Seriously, I feel for you. I would just walk away."

He then got weepy, "She's my first girlfriend. I love her."

And then came Big Boy from the side, with a man-crushing shoulder hug that made Archie wince, "I love you, Archie!"

Archie's world had gone mad.

About a week later, Archie came to work morose and sulking, not even snapping back at the "sissy" insults, caring not enough about his torment to point out how stupid and illiterate his coworkers were as they heckled him. There was not enough juice left in Archie's soul to feed the vampires that surrounded him.

Then, about 2:30 a.m., as the customers who stopped in after closing from the bars shopped for their munchies, Archie's girl came through the door with two men in their mid twenties, one holding each slender hand, who looked to be well-to-do by their clothing. They walked by Archie, seemingly not knowing who he was, or the significance of their presence, as she bought two packs of condoms from Liz.

The joking stopped.

We all knew now that Archie was sulking because he had been dumped.

But this was beyond the pale.

Silverback and Big Boy and Buster looked on angrily at the threesome, even as the Dark Elf shook his head.

Buster said, "I got your back Arch."

Big Boy snarled, menacingly, "We could say them rich boys was steelin,' plant something on them after we whoop dat pretty-boy ass."

Silverback said, open-mouthed, "Ya may be a sissy white faggot, Arch, but dis shid hea ain' right. No man deserve ta be done like dis. I would kill dat bitch."

Archie said softly, as he turned away from his tormentress and began to face up the pickle display with his giant hands, "Thanks guys, but she's already dead to me. And I thought you were the savages."

Postscript

Archie began taking boxing lessons from me, had a few fights, and became a guy that was not picked on. Eventually he got a few promotions outside of the store, and the last time I saw him, when I was working as a vender in another location, he seemed to have matured into a man that lives in his own mind.

'Your Favorite Actresses?'

A Man Question from Edwin

"James, since you are writing two books on dealing with women—at least—I think the readers, such as I, should know what you mean by an attractive woman. Sexual attraction is largely subjective. So, perhaps you could limit your choices to actresses, since we have all seen them. I have no particular number in mind. How about the ones who come to mind?"

Edwin

Okay, Edwin. First off, I do not have relationships with women based on physical appearances, and have declined to date the

most attractive women that have been interested in me, so that I would not end up like Samson or Enkidu.
These actresses will mostly be old, as I developed my taste in such women forty years ago.

As far as actresses go, here are my favorites from least to most:

6. Elizabeth Hurly, based on her slutty movie roles and excellent BMI.

https://www.youtube.com/watch?v=A5x7QQMptSU

5. Ann Margaret, more so when she was in her 40s and 50s than when she was model thin in the 1960s.

https://www.youtube.com/watch?v=VPK5Htf0pv8

4. Scarlett Johansen, in anything tight, is my favorite Nordic babe.

https://www.youtube.com/watch?v=hIu4m91FHDM

3. Rachel Welch, when she did the playboy spread in her 40s, before most of you guys were alive.

https://www.youtube.com/watch?v=cvsQmsj9WVw

2. Sophia Loren, from 18 to 80, particularly in her role in El Cid opposite Charlton Heston, represents my ideal type, similar to Robert E. Howard's ideal of exotic dark-haired white women most often depicted in his Conan stories.

https://www.youtube.com/watch?v=jSNIIuEQq6g

1. The second chick in this clip is a babe named Verna Bloom, who played Clint's love interest in The High Plains Drifter, and reprised the same roll in a C-list rip-off Eyes of a Stranger, of that western, set in modern times, apparently, for no other reason than the lead actor/director, David Heavener, wanted to do a nude scene with her, which Clint had somehow neglected.

https://www.youtube.com/watch?v=RjFuN0OyGzI

In my mind, personality counts for more than looks. My attraction to Hurly and Bloom probably had more to do with their diction than their curves. My pick for most beautiful woman in the world is a 70-year-old waitress from Pittsburg named Punky, who is half Navaho and half Italian, and whose father killed a Jap with meat cleaver at Guadalcanal when his kitchen got overrun near Henderson Field. Recently, when playing scrabble with my mother, my son tried to spell MILF, the definition of which baffled her. I just looked at her and said, "Punky" and she got it right away.

'That Evil Bitch Deserved It'

A Conversation among Men and Males

I was taking my break up front when a regular customer came through. He is a towering man who played college football and pro basketball, and whose son is going into the NBA this year. He is a cabbie that has been threatened and attacked by many of the new generation of sissy black thugs, who all grew up under a mommy's wing and act accordingly, like bitches. He says that's why he's impatient with his own, the young generation, because "they have no grit, no balls, no respect, nothing but bitch in the blood."

Feeling the same way about my own, who were gathered around discussing football, I said nothing. Not right away. He was a Steelers fan and was busting on the Ravens, to howls of disapproval from the staff. Finally, when asked why he disliked the Ravens, he said because it was "prejudice* what they did with Ray Rice. I didn't like the little guy, but they done him wrong."

*It is so nice to hear the term prejudice instead of the deformed catchall "racism."

The other three men went off, talking about how women are sacred, and you can't have an NFL hero punching a woman and hauling her out of the elevator like a sack of laundry. They then -season ticket holders, two of them—pointed out how many people turned their Ray Rice Jersey in at the game when his shirt was recalled. The lone black man in the conversation was just shaking his head, knowing that these sissy, pussy-whipped white fellows would defend their women's opinion at all costs. He was being too kind to bring up the subject of who wore the pants in their family, as many fulltime male retail food employees who are married have a wife who makes more money than they do and therefore calls the shots.

I had to put my two cents in, and his eyes bugged out, not having realized that I was an honorary African American, "First it was a lie—he did not punch her. That was a slap."

My boss said, "But you can't hit a woman that hard. You have to turn the other cheek."

"Dude, I know you've never lain down with a black woman—let alone woke up next to the bitch. She was coming at him like a banshee. The only thing he did wrong is he used the Serena Williams Pimp Slap on her when the Robin Givens Pimp Slap was called for and dropped her ass."

My man was happy, nodding and saying, "And she spit in his face. That is a crime worse than a slap, which is simple battery."

The middle-aged pussy whipped men were wringing their hands and decrying the death of chivalry, and objected to how she was dragged out of the elevator, so I said it, "Not a black woman turned her Jersey in. That was all white women that sent him down to the whipping post, just so you guys would know who was boss. The sisters knew that those high and mighty white bitches were just using Ray to make a point and taking her money in the bargain."

That's when my tag team partner stepped in and said, "Yeah, the man still ain't workin', still on the black list over something that should have stayed between the two of them."

I chimed in, "That evil bitch deserved it!"

The pussy whipped team threw up their hands and said, "There's no reasoning with you guys, you even live in the city," one said as he pointed to me, which earned me the non sissy nod from the big man as he left shaking his head.

One of the things I like about discussing sports—even sports I could care less about—is that men of different races can have heated arguments over these subjects and usually do not let it get personal, which I think is healthy.

At times like this, I am faced with the fact that spiritually and culturally—particularly in relation to my masculine identity—I am much more like a sixty year old black man than is a 40 year old black man, and that middle-aged white men seem to be as distant from me as 20-year-old black men, both very different groups having one common tie, emasculation, and the shamefully apologetic life of the postmodern social eunuch, for all intents and purposes a steer in a pasture where bulls used to run, a pasture now fenced and ruled by the cows.

'After the Nelson'

Columbine Joe #10: Living with A Drama Queen

"The one [girlfriend] who was the bodybuilder, who I put in the full nelson—for which the responding cops complimented me—she was black. It really helped me understand why black guys are the way they are and what they have to put up with. She was just so loud, and would want to get physical any time there was a disagreement—and disagreements sometimes happen in relationships. But the fact that she got loud always brought heat.

"Yes, she tried to hit me with shoes, and books and other things.

"Yes, she tried to stab me—with a pair of scissors mind you.

"Of course, I learned from boxing that the easiest person to deal with in a fight is the person that thinks they can fight, and has no idea what they are doing—which pretty much encompasses black women.

"Well, after the cops who gave me the ataboy on the nelson, it reoccurred, and there is another cop at the door. This cop was a giant Amazon black was one big woman—six and a half feet and two-fifty—all muscle and scowl. The first thing that came through my mind is, 'If she is not gay, I wonder what kind of dude she is with. I mean, he's either Tiny Tim or Mike Tyson. I couldn't imagine anyone in between the two extremes being a fit.'

"Now, I could tell right away that she hated white people, particularly grungy long-haired dudes. She was taking my girl's side. But then my girl starts running her mouth. So she decided not to lock me up. Then she keeps running her mouth and almost got herself locked up.

"Then, the next time she starts screaming and the neighbors call—understandably so—the cops are cool, and they talk to me. But then they pull me aside and say, 'Look, we know what the deal is. It's her. But, she's not getting the results she wants. So one day she's going to say you hit her. And when she makes that claim—even though it will be lie—then we put the cuffs on you and take you away. So do us all a favor and get out of this relationship.'

"I very much appreciated the way they talked to me. So I took their advice and have not crossed that line again. It's just not worth it. Living like that is a ticket to jail. The combative lifestyle just begs for it. When everything is an argument, and any argument can get physical than it all takes you to the same bad place."

'Why Aren't There More Female Villains?'

A Man Question from Malcolm about Writing Fiction

A young black fellow I work with has been writing and running story ideas by me as of late. Recently he became inspired by my novella, Winter and spoke to me at length about this as we sorted our orders last night. His computer is down right now, so he won't be able to read this. Beneath his question is my best recollection of my answer.

"I've been working on this story with my brother and we want to do a female villain. But, is there a reason why there aren't any female villains, and if they are it's the one with the goddess complex, not a Lilith type demoness? Really, the more I think of it its weirding me out, afraid maybe I've missed something. Why aren't there more female villains?"

-Malcolm

"It's simple. Traditionally most authors in your genre [fantasy] have been white men, who have typically worshipped women. Now they are being supplanted by female authors, who worship their feminist self-image. So there is no real reference point for a female villain in the postmodern construct, whose adherents are busy either defying the earth as a cosmic goddess, or reshaping the image of the omniscient deity along less threatening masculine lines. If more black dudes wrote fantasy we'd have more female villains. So put it out there brother—shake up the template."

Malcolm thought long and hard, rubbing his chin, paced nervously for a few seconds, and said, "Yeah, I can see that—but, my mother will probably read it. Now my brother, my brother has had like a million insane bitch girlfriends—

totally off the hook, one more insane than the other. So I'll have him come up with the female villain and I'll write the dialogue!"

» Add a comment «

Jeremy Bentham	November 1, 2015 12:57 PM EST

Here's a real-life example of a female villain for you: a female mad sniper. One Brenda Ann Spencer, age 16. Just cute as a button. She was, in fact, the very first juvenile school shooter in America. In 1979 she murdered two adults and wounded eight children with a .22 caliber rifle. When apprehended her justification for the rampage was "I don't like Mondays".

http://murderpedia.org/female.S/s/spencer-brenda.htm

https://en.wikipedia.org/wiki/Cleveland_Elementary_School_shooting_(San_Diego)

Her case inspired rocker Bob Geldof to compose the song "I Don't like Mondays" for The Boomtown Rats.

https://www.youtube.com/watch?v=8yteMugRAc0

Enjoy!
Bernie Hackett October 29, 2015 6:02 PM EDT

My sympathy to Malcolm's brother. Some of us just draw them.

Perhaps a thinly disguised Mrs. Clinton, pulling her Macbethian strings from the middle of her web of evil?

I like the description as how a SJW sees all us E-vile people. Burn down the friggin' rain forest!

Well, I gotta go kick a puppy.

Later!
Sam October 29, 2015 4:03 PM EDT

This pedastalization of women has slipped its bonds in pursuit of a death wish. Bunch of military wonks are so afraid to tell women to fuck off that they continue to make the military into a place in which no man would want to serve.

F/Small Wars Journal; "Changing the "Macho" Male Culture of the US Military"

Fun quote:

"It isn't really about ending sexual assault; it's about controlling people and changing behavior. Men have the advantage in almost every way, so we have to find ways to cut into that advantage. Making traditional male behavior something that is socially unacceptable will cut their advantage. We have to make it unacceptable for men to talk the way they talk now, act the way they act now, and interact the way they do with women now, and have traditionally." Hyping sexual assault statistics, making women fearful of men, and building a system that finds men guilty until proven innocent are simply means to the greater end of "cutting male advantage."

http://smallwarsjournal.com/jrnl/art/changing-the-%E2%80%9Cmacho%E2%80%9D-male-culture-of-the-us-military

Jeremy Bentham   October 29, 2015 2:04 PM EDT

Yeah that's the ticket! We need more female villains. If women truly want equality in all things then they should get equal time at being the bad guy.

A female villain would be especially implacable and terrifying. One thing I have noticed about bad girls in real life is that not only must they have their way in all things, but everyone else around them must be happy with the fact that they got their way. And say so. They never let up on you. You cannot fight back against them in the same straightforward way you can against than a male opponent. Society expects you to show females forbearance and mercy that you would not be expected to show against a male enemy. That all makes them too scary by far!

Of course that will be a hard sell to a publisher since in today's PC culture you are NEVER supposed to "punch down" and criticize or ridicule officially recognized "oppressed" groups, particularly women. You must ALWAYS "punch up" and criticize or ridicule "privileged" groups, particularly Christian, heterosexual white men. I imagine then for a female villain to be acceptable to the SJWs who control the popular culture she would have to be made very Un-PC and therefore very unlikeable. She would have to be white, blonde, racist, homophobic, an industrialist, a global warming denier and Nazi or KKK. A "BT-1000" on the other hand would probably not be an acceptable villain: "It can't be bargained with. It can't be reasoned with. It doesn't feel pity, or remorse, or fear. And it absolutely will not stop, ever, until you are dead."

JL responds: October 29, 2015 3:01 PM EDT

Yes—the Tyrantess, after her victory, must see that we are glad, and if our idiot grin of bliss wavers...

Dating Duz

On Bitches is Back for White Wednesday!: A Symbiotic Luv Triangle That Could Have Been

Duz was a guy I boxed with back in the 1980s, who is a full-blooded Polish-American with freakish strength and astonishing injury resilience. He is the guy beating me up in The Logic of Force. Although he only weighs about 195 he has retard strength. He once fell from 20 feet in a stock room, onto a pallet of onions, got up, brushed himself off, and went back to work.

He was once hit by a late model Buick while running from two armed robbers. He told me about this in between bench press sets while he pumped weights at the gym a few hours later.

His head was so damned hard that, when we sparred, I used to pray that's he'd finally slip a punch so my hands could heal.

Finally, one day Duz told me he wanted to fight—to go all out to the finish in a boxing match with four once gloves. I agreed, got floored three times, fought off the wall while he body checked me and pounded away [we did this in my concrete basement] for what seemed forever, digging hooks to his body for minutes, never letting him land a clean shot. Eventually I got off the wall, began to circle and jab, and he tapped out, unable to breathe.

I spent three days in bed, with the inside and outside of my arms bruised, and even my ribs bruised from him punching "threw" my arms and smashing them into my body.

Duz, on the other hand, "Got drunk, banged Scaggy Aggie, and went for a five mile run..."

Five years later I met Duz at Tattoo Rick's bar to interview him about his violent life. S. J., my current roommate, was also there. Duz had not seen me since I had let my hair grow down my back, and was inspired by my grungy appearance to tell a tale of lust and concession.

Duz suffers from a full blown case of Jungle Fever, and when he was younger used to drive a hot pink 54 Cadillac. At this point, in 1996, he was driving a big rice burner and managing a ghetto supermarket, which all the black employees thought was his cover for being "an FBI agent or something," since he looked "so ridiculously white and uptight."

"So, I can't date the cashiers—until they get fired. When I fire them—if they qualify—I get their phone number.

"Liked this one girl.

"Waited a few days and called.

"She says she'd love to go out, but needed money for a baby sitter.

"'Noooo, problem—be right over.'

"She meets me at the door, dolled up, kids playing with some tall, skinny, greasy, long-haired white guy.

"I give her the money.

"She walks over to Dude and gives it to him.

"I said, 'Who is that?'

"She said, 'That's the babies' daddy.'

"I said, 'I'm not paying any man to watch his own kids!'

"She says, 'He won't watch them unless I pay him.'

"Then Dude gets up off the couch, steps over this low ceramic tile or marble coffee table and pushes me with one hand—which does nothing—and tells me to leave.

"Forearm smash to the chest—he flies back over the coffee table.

"I step over [Duz just grabs my long hair and balls it up in his meaty fist as I notate] and start punching the face, haven't beat the shit out of anyone in a long time—feeling reeeeeeal good.

"Then she jumps on my back and starts screaming and hitting me, so I reversed grip on his hair and began smashing the face into the coffee table—ooooh yeah! Then, I walk away, shake her off and walk out the door—and here I sit, fucking feeling right!"

[I was now leaning back over the bar as he snarled in my face and twisted my hair.]

S.J. spoke up, "Hey, Duz, so did you get your money back?"

Duz let go of my hair and looked confusedly at S.J. and, after a moment, confessed, "No, I forgot all about it until now."

S.J. continued, "So, would you say beating that guy up was worth the money you lost?"

"Hell yes!" snarled Duz.

S.J. crowned the interview he had hijacked with, "Well, then maybe you ought to call her back and set up another date. I'm sure the money was worth the beating he took. You three could develop a symbiotic relationship."

» Add a comment «
TheRedSkull November 25, 2015 9:29 PM EST

Kipling can't exist today

Colonialism has gone gay.

Now the fellow's James LaFond

Slumming in a negroid pond.

The Bitch Test

How Emasculated Are You?

You go to the pharmacy to get a script filled and the pharmacist, who has no other customers, and is free to slide your Z-PAC of antibiotics off the shelf and into your hand, informs you that he may not complete your transaction for another 20 minutes, for it is company policy. This is, of course, the policy of pharmacies and supermarkets with pharmacies, who need to pay the rent and thus want you to support their bid to stay in business and continue employing low-IQ slackers, by buying your tea bags and honey from them while your order is "being processed."

Do you:

A. Conclude the first phase of the transaction in such a way as to insure good honest treatment from this pharmacist in the future and then go next door to grab a pint, a salad, a babe, a game of pool, etc.

B. Stew angrily over the injustice done you by the money grubbing retailer's policy.

C. Rail at the pharmacist, complain, and /or try to get them to make an exception in your case.

D. Stung by the injustice of this policy you seek to convince the retailer to change its policy for the greater good and devote yourself to a letter-writing, phone-calling, blogging, face-booking and politicking campaign to convince the retailer to change its evil ways.

E. Understanding that the true root of this evil imposition upon your health is beyond the scope of 'the market' you campaign to have a law passed that will bar drug sellers with other goods to sell from making a customer wait for the customary length time.

How Did You Score?
A. Man: You are a tactically thinking man who deals with the world rather than call for the

world to change. If you were a Paleolithic hunter you would not waste time beseeching the gods to remove the claws and teeth from rival predators or whine into the uncaring sky that it is unfair that stags bound so swiftly over the heather while you must creep, stalk and wait in order to kill them, because the sky is your daddy and should provide for you...

B. Civilized Man: Your natural tactical mindset has been so submerged in the corrupt crybaby incubator of weakness that is Civilization, that you waste valuable energy and mental powers on bringing your anger under control. If you were a Paleolithic hunter that reacted with anger when a bison turned out to be swifter than the run of the herd, you would be left biting your lip while better men adjusted to the situation and brought down the beast that would feed the clan for a moon—while you sulked and were therefore left comforting yourself with your calloused hand while they laid with the grateful women...

C. Drone: You are the tittering disposable insect of the great hive, pining to mate with and be eaten headfirst by the merciless queen. If you were a member of a Paleolithic tribe you would be left at home with the women and children, denied mating rights, and your pathetic genes would embrace oblivion...

D. Bitch: You are a bitch. If you were a member of a Paleolithic society you would be made to live as a woman, and every time you opened your mouth to complain about something there would therein be a reproductive device inserted to muffle your irritating babble.

E. Psychobitch: You are the most savage and unpleasant type of female imitator, that upon which the progress of the hive mind is built. Your inability to deal with anything in its natural state and condition has resulted in your unholy yearning to change the world and mould it into something you can easily manage. If you were a goddess the altars of your priests would run red. If you were a member of a Paleolithic band you would be ostracized and left in the wilderness for the night spirits to deal with, your plaintive shrieking preserved by the mournful Wind as she wailed over the waste to remind future generations of women of the fate of she who complains inconsolably.

» Add a comment «

Sam J. December 16, 2015 9:52 PM EST

I don't think I've ever had this happen. I would just go somewhere else. If the bison are not in the field why stay there?

O Hayes December 16, 2015 6:05 PM EST

I do F. Unless I'm dying the prescription can wait. So i just drop it off and pick it back up whenever i'm passing back by. Fuck meds anyway

Hank A December 16, 2015 5:09 PM EST

Wow.... does anybody even consider options b-e? It seems like lunacy

Goose December 16, 2015 1:47 PM EST

Some other options I've used:

A+: develop a personal connection with the pharmacist (and try convincing him to bend the store policy when no one is around)

F: use an independent pharmacy that doesn't have the money-grabbing policy

G: stay healthy and not use any drugs, especially for sickness that the body/immune system can handle on its own - colds, flus, muscle aches etc.

How would they translate to the Paleolithese?

Sean December 16, 2015 1:13 PM EST

Ha just had this happen actually. I chose to play games with my 3 year old until the time had passed.

'No Woman Would Ask to Be Disrespected'

'I Know Because I am A Woman': A Man Challenge from Janine

"James, I like you fiction—a lot. But, in the interest of realism, and you do write in a realistic vein, I must inform you, that no woman would ask a man to "disrespect her," even if she went in for rough stuff. I know because I am a woman. Keep up the good work, stay crazy, and if you need any more tips on what goes on inside of a woman's head, just e-mail me."

-Janine

Thanks for the compliment, Janine, and also congratulations on knowing the erotic terminology of all 4 billion of your sisters. This is of great interest to me. I have never had a male reader write in and say, "No man would ever do this, or say that, ever," because us guys know that there are dudes that will do and say anything, including asking to be disrespected with a pink whippy-wand.

However, all of the most intelligent women I know, some a good deal smarter than I, have, at some point or another, made such an absolute statement, some not limited to women, but discussing men in combat. Leigh once said, "Jay could have never survived that injury, even if he is a genetically engineered super soldier."

However, the injury in question was survived by a woman I knew, who continued to scream and fight, and she was no super soldier!

This need for every woman to be the same, and in some cases for the woman to wish that all men, or all people are the same, seems ingrained in female kind. All of my female editors have this sense, and all object to me thinking that I can write about a woman's feelings and what she would do in this situation or that, what her sexual limits are, etc.

So, Janine you know, with absolute accuracy, that Janine would never ask a man to disrespect her, even if Janine desperately wanted some man to disrespect her. I believe that, get it, and understand it. I also have personal standards.

So, when "Big Titty" Tanyika wagged her G-cups at me and snarled playfully, "Mista' Jimmy, I wan ya ta disrespect dese, den disrespect da shit outta what dey attached to," I was a bit taken aback. Now, as much as Mister Jimmy may have been into giant, disembodied, milk chocolate, teenage, breastessez begging for discipline under his firm didactic hand, he had to pause at the prospect of getting intimate with someone who would just come out and say such a thing, in public, with Pete working the produce rack ten feet away.

Just before I broke up with this one psycho-bitch for the 17th [Okay, it may have been the 23rd time for all I know.] time, while declining a sexual opportunity because I was suffering from a severe concussion and the room was spinning, she said, "Get over it, sissy boy, and give me the disrespect I deserve."

And, last, but not least, while discussing general work subjects with a married female coworker—a boss, actually—I made the empathetic point to ask her how she was doing, to which she responded, "I'd be doing a lot better if I could get disrespected every once in a while, up to and including gagging...though I draw the line at having my head bounced off the dashboard."

Janine, I am a man of honor, even where indiscretions long past are concerned. So I leave it to you to figure out which of the three requests to be disrespected I honored.

Thanks for checking in, and stay thirsty, my friendess!

'My Bitch'

Tia, the Twerp and White Daddy

In the following dialogue with a coworker you will notice a common theme that I deal with concerning black women and their drones and white women 35 and younger, the gender role reversal. There is also the very female-like terms of discussion and behavior exhibited by increasing numbers of middle-aged white men, who sound, more and more, in their workplace discussions, like the women of my mother's generation, inveterate gossips.

Tia: "Hey, Mister Jimmy."

Mister Jimmy: "How is it goin,' Tia?"

Tia: "You know, Mister Jimmy, you told me how it was gonna be when I got this promotion."

Mister Jimmy: "I told you you'd never be half the bitch that little twerp is."

Tia: "Oh, you know that's right! He on vacation now, which is well and good, but he has spent the last two weeks telling me what he was going to be doin' sexing that little junkie girl a his. This is honeymoon week in the ghetto. You got a fitty-year-ole man, but five feet tall, with no teeth and a bald head, with a twenty-five-year-old junkie who done dropped three black babies out a her ass and the State or baby daddy's mamma got custody of all three, en you gonna tell me that ain't about sex or money. All he can talk about is the sex—just like a woman talk all the time on her man."

Mister Jimmy: "He actually names sex acts and discusses what they do?"

Tia: "Yes sir, Mister Jimmy, especially when I'm filling the cream-filled doughnuts! It is disgusting. A course you know what it's about when you see her little white snow bunny self en know she been dropping black babies. I mean, you living with a man twice your age who you just met and not payin' bills, you know what that's about. Excuse me, but that's about suction! That girl could suck the lava out of a dormant volcano—and that ain't no lie! And that's okay—that's his life. But why do I have to hear about all of the gooey details at work. And then, after I work for him all week while he getting' his freak on and playing STD roulette—cause you just know he bare backin' that!—he has to come back in here and complain about the work I do, and my work's fine. I mean, I may not be able to suck the lava out of a volcano, but I sure as heck can bake some bread!"

Mister Jimmy: "Look, your work is good, your boss is happy. Just ignore him."

Tia: "I know I should, but then he starts picking on me—like a woman do, telling me how my man don't work, and he's just using me, and I better put a lock on the beer cooler when I'm at work. I'm doin' the best I can. I don't depend on no man. My ex-husband doesn't make his child support. But you don't see me being a bitch and goin' to White Daddy [the government] to get my money. I work my two jobs and I control the money I make. The plantation is closed—White Daddy can take care of all those hos who need they fake hair."

Mister Jimmy: "So, essentially, you are living as the white men of my generation lived. You are the bread-winning head-of-household."

Tia: "That's right. I didn't spread my legs to get a roof over my head."

Mister Jimmy: "So, you're not bothered about him gossiping on you like a woman, but about him talking down to you as a head-of-household, of putting on airs that he has his house in order and that you do not?"

Tia: "Exactly!"

Mister Jimmy: "Then, woman to "man," what are you going to say to that little twerp next time he breaks bad with you about your boyfriend?"

Tia grinned widely, looking down at me from her great height, and said, "I'll tell him, 'At least My Bitch don't suck dicks!' when he needs to get high, but just snatches a beer out of the cooler."

James LaFond, reporting from the heart of your Emasculation Nation

» Add a comment «

B February 20, 2016 2:21 PM EST

Gross.

Is it just me or do black women have contempt for mud sharks (beyond the "you stealing our men" thing) more or less the same way that white supremacists do?

On a tangentially related note, a drunken monkey attacks bar patrons with a knife in Brazil: https://youtu.be/mfKGWAivpkA

http://www.israelnationalnews.com/News/News.aspx/208290#.Vsi7Tvl95D8

Jim, could you analyze the monkey's technique and poise? On one hand, the monkey is holding the knife in an icepick grip, an indicator of murderous intent. On the other hand, he does not seem to be very committed.

JL responds: February 21, 2016 10:17 AM EST

Thanks for the link!

Black women are a mixed bag on this one.

The top echelon are happy to let the snow bunnies keep the black men while they hunt for a white knight.

The working class girls like Tia think that mud sharks are wretched.

Your BT-1000s regularly beat up mud sharks and compete with them.

This knife attack deserves an article!

'To Destroy the Masculine Enigma'

Feminazi Bitch: By Proctor Testosterone, AKA, 'Bitches Still Call'

Last night, over dinner, my august Co-Author and doctor of wench-kind, discussed plans for expanding our co-authorship of the "Manly Manual on the Enemy Sex." Here he presents one of the many acidic fruits that ripened during that discussion.

"You don't have to hold the door for me because I am a woman," she accused, as she snickered in her repressive bitch mode.

Oh, this would be a good day for a bitch session. In front of me the bitch. Her opponent: a Neanderthal that was taught by his father to be a man, a real man. Not the "man" of our current time. You know, the emasculated, metro sexual pussy who hides and runs from his evolutionary physical supremacy because he has allowed a misguided, weak, liberal society to destroy the masculine enigma.

Seriously, did she really say that to me? I mean, I have read about "women" like this, but I honestly did not think that such creatures actually existed. Unfortunately, she was emphatically real and now nauseatingly lecturing me on the new world feminazi order.

"I am not holding the door for you because you are a woman. I am holding the door for you because I am a gentleman," came the reply of the real man.

BOOM! Yes, bitch, that was my response. Smoke on that fragrance of insanity.

What, a gentleman? Well, arguably with the use of my offensive terminology associating the female dog to the fairer sex might justifiably question the classification. Good Lord, I was just holding the door. I do it for everyone. It is the nice thing to do. And YES, I go out of my way to do it for a woman, any woman, because it is the right thing to do.

Real men, gentlemen—men who are psychologically powerful enough to be physically and socially gentle—treat women and everyone with respect. They express that respect in direct action by saying, "Hey, I place you first because I value you as a person and a woman."

You see, real men value women because they are just that, WOMEN! There is no hidden motive or alternative agenda in the simple act. It is what it is as a sign of respect. Even if that respect is undeserving for such a disgusting, confused femme fatale.

For a brief moment I debated in my caveman mind to just move on and let things be. But she would not allow such civility and continued her vociferous barrage of bullshit and feminist propaganda aimed vehemently at her knight in black sweats and baseball cap.

"Jesus, woman, I was just being nice. Stop reading into it."

Well, any attempt to rationalize with this tigress of disdain fell to the bowels of caveman hell. She was relentless. Relentless with a B, and an I..........TCH!

"What, you think because I am a woman I need special treatment?"

"No, for Christ's sake, I thought we established my proclivity for civility and chivalry."

Apparently I forgot the cardinal rule for some of today's "women." Any visible display of a distinction of the sexes is a no-no. Yeah, it's bad. Well, at least for some. Hmmmm, let me get this straight. Treating a woman like a woman is somehow anti-woman. Yep, you got it. Gestate on that for a while during your caveman meal of gnawing on your latest kill and satisfying your gastrointestinal primitive urges.

Crap, and she was rather hot by most standards. Given a different scenario I would have clubbed her in the head and towed her gnarly ass back to the bat cave for some head board banging and hedonistic screams of passion. In my testosterone override and physiologic state of perpetual penile priapism I was misled by the smaller head. Women know that is a man's weakness. Even if it is a stereotype. That is part of our evolution too. Well, my statement of unbridled manliness was not taken well.

"Listen, Honey, in another setting I would have asked you to possibly have a drink and perhaps later even come home to my abode. Perhaps if you were comfortable with your own sexual identity you might have considered it, both of us being mildly attracted to one another."

Well, being the caveman I was, I intentionally fooled my fragile mind to believe she might be oozing estrogen attraction to match my thirst for sexual conquest. Alas, a gentleman is always honest with women and himself, even a caveman-gentleman. A gentleman also does not lower his standards regardless of hotness for a bitch of a woman who doesn't even accept or like the pure fact of her own gender. That is how the bitch evolved. She progressively denied her own identity as a woman in order to emasculate the masculine half of the species. Since that is actually easier than accepting truth and distinction of difference between the sexes.

It is actually simple, quite simple. The feminazi's hate themselves. They won't or can't admit this state of self-hatred. It is no different than the excessively emasculated, feminized, pseudo-male who similarly hates himself. Thus they take on the roles of the opposite gender. So it is easier to accept some false sense of security basked in the pseudo crap of liberal progressivism that says there is no difference between the sexes. Men can act like women, and women can act like......well, whatever the hell they think they are acting like.

You see, I don't get offended when you hold the door for me. I am not somehow stripped of my guy card by your act of civility. I am secure in my manliness and my role in society, the family and the interaction of the human sexes. But all things being unequal, I will always hold the door for you. Because my gentlemen gene propagates that insane, irrational behavior.

Well, sorry to burst your vaginal bubble ladies, but there are multiple necessary evolutional distinctions between the sexes. We are not the same. WE NEVER will be. Billions of years have forced such a development. You should be grateful for that development. You should be grateful for gentlemen. You should be grateful for these differences. Otherwise, we would have no development or be here for that matter.

As much as the feminazi bitch lived in her selected offense, her projection of her own disgust with herself towards that which exposes her disgust is her own downfall. And this exposes her hypocrisy in shining, estrogenized glory.

Really, the simple act of holding a door is so offensive?

The purity, nicety, and decency of respect is offensive. Apparently so. And this is exactly why you are and will remain a bitch. Now, that is offensive. It is meant to be.

There is no "I" in team. The team is the human race, the daily play and interaction of men and women being nice to one another. The team is me the man, and you the woman, talking, flirting, exposing ourselves towards a more intimate interaction. Interaction.....it begins with "I." I, me, you. Well, there is no "I" in team. But there is one in BITCH.

NO, I am not holding the door for you because you are a woman. Actually, your expressive disdain and bitchiness to my action decrease my sense of your distinction as a woman. BUT, even if you are a bitch, regardless, you are still deserving of my chivalry and gentlemanly act. So I will always hold the door for you, even if you are not coming back to my cave for screaming pleasure. I am holding the door for you because that is what men do. Even for you, the bitch!

» Add a comment «

Ishmael March 11, 2016 11:43 AM EST

It's also a great way to check out their booty, if they go first, sunglasses on of course to protect my blue eyes.

Thank You, Jacob

We Appreciate the Support

Jacob, while we appreciate your enthusiasm, please do not get carried away. If you happen to find a stray virgin wandering witless and lost in the asphalt jungle, do not attempt to sacrifice her to the God of Thunder. Appeasing his Bolt-hurling Omnirotica is a job for a professional, such as myself. Hire a Salvadoran gangster or Mormon Elder to transport her to White Avenue in Harm City, Maryland, and set her loose. Never fear, I will find her when I hear Raeaynalita two doors down shout, "Oh, no she didn't walk down da mufafucin' street in 'er own hair in fron' a ma manz!"

As the hoodrats begin testing the breeze with their flaring nostrils and circling on their stolen bikes, converging on her position, I promise to effect a news-worthy rescue!

Thanks again, Jacob.

Macho Nachos

Your Low Budget Wingman

Are you an urban dude expecting a visit from a suburban babe?

Is this babe likely to return—of course she is, as soon as you train the bitch out of her!

Then, offer to cook. Say, "Baby, I've got dinner on the stove—just come straight over. I don't want you spending time or money feeding me. I just want you."

Of course that's complete bullshit, other than the fact that your cluttered microwave top can be loosely defined as a stove top.

When she arrives, put on the meal, a plate of nachos. Babes love nachos. Even bitches love nachos.

Use the authentic border jumper favorite, Charras sea salt and Chile Limon flavored tortillas, bought in the ethnic food aisle frequented by Latino construction workers.

Cover liberally with whatever kind of cheese Mister Mike has marked down for being close dated down at the ghetto grocery. Feta cheese is best, as chicks like it but will be so salty with these chips that they will be nigh unconsumable by a woman, especially one worried about retaining fluid!

She will eat enough to get thirsty but still be hungry.

Trust me, I tried this recently and it has the two desired effects.

First she will get really thirsty and with you having nothing to drink but beer, emotional lubrication and a resignation as to her purpose will soon overcome her.

Secondly, this babe will never again show up at your door without a home-cooked meal!

You are set, bro. One box of condoms [$4.99] and a bag of chips [$3.19] for under 10 dollars should net you three dedicated cooks for as long as you can juggle them.

Oh, and don't forget your ownership manual:

Bro, buy this book and it's only a matter of time before the bitch queens that have ruined your life will have their hairstyle altered to accommodate your beer coaster!

http://www.amazon.com/Your-Trojan-Whorse-Manual-Ownership/dp/1530922879/ref=sr_1_6/187-1557997-7690221?s=books&ie=UTF8&qid=1460048512&sr=1-6&keywords=james+lafond

Being White Daddy

Comportment in the Face of Imminent Emasculation

When, in the year after my birth, the men who ruled this nation decided to destroy the black family by putting all the power into the hands of single women, a race was called back onto the plantation of the mind, their bodies were let loose to clear working class areas for eventual gentrification. As this outward burning anti-cultural brushfire cleanses the body politic and the elite savor the thought of reoccupying the city center, their female minions do their bidding, by producing the least psychologically able male children possible.

Below are two examples from this past week:

First [this has happened to me on my street twice this year] I was walking down to the market past a car with two open doors that was parked in front of a rental house. Standing next to the passenger-side door was a 25-year-old woman. In the back seat was a child. Standing next to the driver's-side door was her man.

He had a "what do you want me to do?" look of asking depression on his open countenance, his hands proffered high and out to the side in the attitude of one who is pleading a hopeless case.

She wore a scowl of disdain and sneered, "Muthafucka, yer shit is jus' pathetic."

He seemed hurt as she turned away from him and looked up into my face, beamed a big pretty smile and said, "God morning, sir."

Being a benevolent white daddy, I tipped my cap and smiled as I returned her good morning. I was not three paces past the car when she lit back into him, "Muthafucka, who you think you tryin' ta impress—bitch!"

He has my pity.

The Apple of My Evil Eye

Last night, in a Baltimore area supermarket, a 35-year-old woman, with her 18-year-old son in tow was watching her food stamp order being rung out at the register when her son asked permission to buy an apple, which was given with a curt nod and a wide eye, hand on hip. The apple turned out to cost an entire dollar and she said, "Oh hell no! I ain' payin' no dolla fo no muvafucin' apple—you feel me boy!"

The full grown man then returned to the produce department to find a better priced apple, and returned with an entire bag of apples that only cost $1.49. As soon as mamma saw this bag of apples she screamed, "Muthafuca, I ought ta whoop yo trifflin' ass! Watch you tryan' ta spend all a my food stamps?"

Mamma screamed at, cussed, degraded and threatened her son for a minute or so and then sent him back to return the purchase. When the white male cashier asked her if he should total the order, she looked up at him, batted her eyes, smiled, called him sir and thanked him graciously.

That is how you build an emasculation nation, one bitch at a time.

Wacsh You Gonna Do!?

I Paid Fo It!

Hoodrat news flash!

Have you wondered why black men are so unhappy?

3:30 p.m. in the afternoon.

At the Ghetto Grocer a very fine looking black woman was shopping with her good looking black man in new fitted cap and sneakers. He was asking "like a sissy" for yogurt and his slave mistress went off!

She was up in his face, chest to chest, in a fighting posture.

"You pussy-ass mothafuca asking for some Hello Kitty yogurt. [the 4-pack strawberry, kind, a hoodrat favorite] You ain't nothin' but a child, not even a man. You ain't even a man muthafuca."

The man said, "Girl. I'm gonna be goin' back to jail."

She responded in a thunderous tone, "Then you be callin' you mammy, not me."

At this point he was smacked and his gold grille cut his lips. He stayed quiet, as the black female customers and staff laughed and made fun of him for being "a pussy" and she ranted, over and over and over again, "I paid fo it! Wash you gonna do!? Nothin' thas wacsh you gonna do cause you notin' but a pussy. You ain' even a man!"

The white women that heard this were surprised that he did not hit her and were convinced that she was trying to get him locked up. The white women thought he behaved admirably with self control, while the black women thought he behaved like a "sissy" and that the female was correct, that since she supports him and pays his way she can do what she wants, including "busting his face" as one older black woman put it.

The men remained silent—even the security guard kept his silence as the ebony queen of this emasculation nation waxed wroth in her indignation.

This is the End of Masculine Time, which will hopefully implode and usher in a new age of manliness.

» Add a comment «
guest April 17, 2016 5:05 AM EDT

Off topic, you will like this:

https://alfinnextlevel.wordpress.com/2016/04/15/how-to-get-more-production-from-your-female-workers-and-slaves/

And sorry to repeat myself, but how many percent, would you say James, of blacks earn their living working in the above ground private sector, is it even 10%?

My rough calculation is that around 30% of working age black men are in prison, 30% are on the dole, 30% have government quota or aa jobs, leaving only around 10% or less in the real free market economy.

What's your quick math on that? Thanks!

Sorry, man, I was down at the seraglio, inspecting the new bitches...

Caramel Cruel

Driving Miss Degeneracy

A story from an Uber driver.

Paddington is an Englishman of Nigerian extraction who drives an Uber car in Baltimore. Yesterday he related the following Friday night drive story.

An attractive young lady, wearing very little clothing, who he thought was dressed in a manner that reminded him of a prostitute, insisted on sitting in the front seat with him. She then went on to regale him about the fact that she had a regular boyfriend, who well knew, that at this very moment, she was being driven across town to have sex with another man.

Paddington was fairly disgusted and was becoming increasingly critical of his decision to drive an Uber car in Baltimore. Earlier that night he had driven woman to a housing project and found she had passed out drunk in the back. He nervously spent a half hour attempting to wake her as "groups of big black men" walked by, regarding him and the woman with interest.

He was further disgusted by the level of detail this college age woman was willing to go into as to the particulars of her upcoming tryst. Eventually—finally!—he pulled up to the destination and the eager boyfriend was waiting his lady love. As if to be certain that this man would also have cause to stew in a well of jealousy, the girl then embraced Paddington most suggestively, told him how much she had enjoyed his conversation and then left him with a longing touch.

Have you ever wondered why so many black dudes are stabbing and beating each other?

Just as black women enjoy raising children to hate the police and then direct them to fight the police, so that they can spend all of their welfare on hair extensions while Junior is in

Juvenile Hall, black women also love to see men fight and die for their attention. There are many reasons for never dating black woman, and this is probably number one, because she is going to start seeing you while living with another guy and is going to tell him all about you.

The Vaginal Vote

Miss Ezz on the Upcoming Presidential Infection

My monthly touching base phone call to the cashier that set off the alarm for last year's Purge turned political today. The charming thing about speaking with Miss Ezz is these phone conversations occur outside of a ghetto supermarket, where she is almost always interrupted, within her 10-minute conversation window, by someone asking for change, the time, a light, a smoke, a date, or directions.

"I really am fascinated by the Trump candidacy, him being the first non-politician since Perot to run. At a certain point the media jumped on Perot and got rid of him, but they've been on Trump all along and he is still hanging in there. He has some smart people working for him. But I don't think they're smart enough to lay on the female vote, which is a must. Look, I'm a woman, and I'm telling you that women vote on looks and charm in the case of male candidates and for the candidate with a vagina in the case of a mixed gender race.

"Trump needs the vaginal vote and he does not seem inclined to compromise his position—which is admirable—to get it. If you don't get the vaginal vote someone else will, because women are stupid and easily led—No, not you sister. No, not that one—the other one right there. You got it baby. Take that into Mister Ron and he'll tell you what to do with it—back at you, Sugar Pumps, you know it's a sea of stupid bitches we're drowning in out here, don't you?"

"Of course you do—later, Shug."

The Genghis Khan Strip Mall

"Dude, if you won a two-hundred million power-ball, what would you do?"

-Steevo Bristol

Thanks for the opportunity, Steevo, to shock the world with my moral complexity!

1. Quit work.

2. Quit coaching.

3. Quit writing.

4. Watch Uncle Sam take 100 million.

5. Give my youngest son [the one with a finance degree]10 million to take care of friends and family.

6. Fight a bull Bison with a boar spear in a rodeo pen.

7. If I survive that, eat the bison with my friends and save the femur bone.

8. Fight a large male leopard in a cage with the bison femur.

9. If I survive that, I will take 90 million and use it to acquire the same bipedal baubles Genghis Khan would treat himself to after making a pyramid of 90-thousand skulls—shopping for slave girls, Bro, at the strip mall below. How many of these could I bag with 90 million? A few, at least.

10. PS: any of them who score 100-plus on the IQ test will be bred—relentlessly.

Genghis Khan's Strip Mall
https://www.youtube.com/watch?v=R9d18SLznZU

» Add a comment «
Ishmael April 28, 2016 5:57 PM EDT

I agree, with the exception of #6 and #8, having killed a bison with a rifle. 3 shots 175 grain Nosler partition close range, 20yds first shot, lungs, through the jaw, second shot, running shot, 3 broke shot the neck, I sent a video concerning the leopard, God speed! Ishmael.

Ronald April 28, 2016 4:53 PM EDT

James please take some of your readers shopping with you.

JL responds: April 28, 2016 4:55 PM EDT

That's one wing man.

Nerds, Knuckleheads, Twerps & Bitch Queens

Notes on Social Intelligence

Dealing with fighters, coworkers, employers and antagonists in street situations, I rely almost exclusively on social intelligence to keep these situations under control. Sometimes for my good, sometimes for the good of my fighters, and on occasion, even for the good of criminals if it also serves to make my marginal day run somewhat smoother. Anyone involved in general reading from the 1980s and 90s will be familiar with the concept of emotional intelligence and men being more logical and analytical and women being more emotional and in tune - the whole Women are from Venus and Men are from Mars bullshit, which really amounts to the fact that Mars was designed to rape Venus, with Venus being adapted to making sure that this was at least a profitable experience on her part.

In dealing with men my age and older, you generally have three types:

1. The logical guy who can never figure out women and can't deal with people from cultures that don't hold the same values as his and is served up with a surprise divorce by his hitherto obedient and compliant wife, who metamorphosed into Medusa with no warning whatsoever, and is then mugged by a panhandler on the way to his attorney's office. We need this guy to build bridges, rocket ships, to let us know how much money we have in our mutual fund, but don't let him make a fight for you—Don King would own him in 15 minutes—and don't expect him to be able to apply any advice that you give him on dealing with the bitch queens that run his life.

2. The impulsive guy, basically a dangerous hairy woman with a dick, whom you could teach how to fight, can have a good time with, but

can't expect him to show up on time for his work out or make a deal with a manipulative type without getting screwed. Chicks like this guy because he thinks he's in charge and they know they are in charge.

3. This is the new version of the impulsive guy, a young emasculated dude who lacks all the emotional intelligence of the logical guy and has had the impulsiveness of the other dude turned into a womanly emotiveness. This guy is hard to deal with because he thinks like the logical guy but gets upset like a woman.

Note that all three of these guys are victim types, none of them able deal with the conniving bitch queen or even initially recognize her. Also note that I didn't put the manipulator on the list. That's because I don't like being a segment of a target population.

The manipulator, or the survivor, or the leader, the alpha man or the taboo omega male, are none of these three but are people who have integrated characteristics of numbers one and two into a survivable behavior package. In other words, the logical guy has to think you're the impulsive guy, if he's going to give up on that game so that you can arrive at a mutual accommodation. The impulsive guy needs to feel like you're the logical guy, so that he can accept your advice and be confident that you're not just a knucklehead like he is. This is the hybrid role of the coach who has to be able to go between the impulsive fighter and the logical manager/promoter so that both parties' interests can be served without the fighter going off the rails or the manager/promoter taking undue advantage of the fighter. Learning how to work a situation like this is no different than running a negotiation between labor and management. Also, managing interactions with criminals is often simply a matter of identifying whether the individual criminal is of the impulsive or logical variety, and in the case of a group of criminals, having an immediate sense of who's management and who's labor.

In terms of women, that's a whole different game. This article is really about dealing with other men in the context of them being in the clutches of some type of woman. As you can see, the problem person here is number three, this new type of emasculated nerd person who gets thrown into a tizzy just like a woman in a movie from the 1950s in the face of any impulsive masculine characteristics. Indeed, if you look at young men and women together these days, you largely see an impulsive female dominating the emasculated male, whether it's a brother and sister, a date, or simply two coworkers interacting.

I personally have to be very careful interacting with this type of male as they are more testosterone-sensitive than women. You see, the woman is really hoping that you're going to have sex with her, and unless this guy is a homo, he wants nothing to do with that, so is repelled. I haven't worked it out for myself yet with the young guys at work, still cringing in fear any time I give a good morning or express a direct opinion. However, I have a suspicion that this is the new version of the logical guy, and there's got to be a way to reach him, although I've probably gone too far down my own knucklehead rabbit hole to have any hope of affecting such a détente myself.

As it stands, the young women their age are more like guys were when I was coming up and are more easily related to, which leads me to the thought that my being sought out for companionship is an expression of a wider phenomenon, which includes some of my friends who are involved with much younger women who will have nothing to do with guys their age. I have no intention of troubling myself with such young vixens unless I win the power ball lottery and buy controlling interests in the Miss Bum Bum Brazil Pageant. But what do we call these old guys who are being sought by young women, not as sugar daddies but as hairy bodies to grind upon and a deep voice to listen to? If all the older women I have dated in my life were, as the term goes, cougars, would not these fellows be known by reference to the same animal, otherwise known as a puma (Latino), a panther (black dude), or a catamount (the BIG mountain lions)?

If we could adopt the above suggested naming scheme, it might once again be a prideful state of being to be a white-bearded, hairy-backed paleface.

Baby, just call me White Daddy.

'The Cake Boy'

Negrodamus on Kicking Shorty to the Curb

Mister LaFond, in our gaming group there are these two eighteen-year-old boys—good dudes. The one is banging all kind of bitches, while the other just kicked his shorty to the curb. From what I heard from him, she was a good girl, cute, pleasant, making nice.

Here he decided that he wants a better car. He had an okay car, but wanted a much better one. I was proud of him that he traded in all of his collectable cards and other boy stuff for the money to get this car. But then he goes and kicks his shorty to the curb, because he said he was spending too much time with her, and too much money on her. I'm like, "Boy, the hand is never as good as pussy and when you have some good pussy why would you trade it in for the hand."

He gonna show up to play cards with a sprained wrist before the summer out if he don't line up some pussy. Mister LaFond, am I right? The hand doesn't cut it—pussy is where it is at. Here I am, after the breakup, trying to retool and get back into the shorty seat and he's throwing pussy away! And it's not like he has more pussy, like the other boy. I could understand kicking an expensive shorty to the curb when you bangin' all kind a bitches.

Now I am beginning to worry about this boy. Him and this other dude he works with are goin' to the ball game together and doin' all kind of other stuff. I wouldn't be surprised if we turned around a year from now and he is coming out of the closet announcing that he a cake boy. Now, I'm cool with cake boys. I'm not into what they into, but can be friends nonetheless. In fact, I recently had need of a cake boy.

I was looking to buy some lingerie for my wife at Victory Secret. My female friends were all either busy or were with jealous dudes. So I went to my cake boy friend and said, "Hey, Armon I need a feminine point of view. Cold you help me out?"

He was cool with it. So we go to Victory Secret and who is waiting on us but another cake boy! It was hilarious, the way these two were carrying on. The more so because the dude thought I was a cake boy, because I was with a cake boy and he gave me a twenty-percent discount. Then, after the purchase, the cake boy says, "Who are you getting this for? It won't fit either one of you."

Who knows, maybe he thought he could fit into it. I looked right at him and said, "This is an anniversary present for my wife."

Oh, the look on his face was priceless. I knew right then that he only gave me the discount because he thought I was a cake boy. When we walked out of there he was flaming angry. But what's he going to do, actually announce that discounts are only for the cake boy?

Among Sniveling Kind

Preface to a A Brief Primer on Leashing Bitches and Running Bitch-Boys

Yesterday, a good friend who forever suffers the slings and arrows of his wench, in keeping with his loyalty to American cultural standards, seemed bemused that I would not ever tolerate a woman raising her voice to me, saying, "No wonder you are not with someone—they have to yell at you, it's part of the deal."

No deal here.

Stranger, nun, teacher, employer, lover, it matters not, a woman who raises her voice to me no longer deserves my company, protection, service of even tolerance, and so I have ever and always walked away. This took some conditioning, but I had it down by the time I was a teen after seeing how poorly verbal engagement with a female worked for my rather savvy father.

Once you have acclimated yourself to this standard of intolerance, when a woman disrespects you it is as if an icy waterfall washed over your soul and you become free.

This generalizes well to dealing with men. For all men who raise their voice to you do so out of weakness. Even if it is a cop, military officer or coach, the raising of the voice represents their evoking of the greater power of the organization in their cause. Therefore, when a man raises his voice to you he has exposed his bitch-parts-which you have hopefully eradicated from your soul—and opened himself up for dismantling at your ruthless hands.

The various aspects of leashing bitches and running bitch-boys will be examined more closely in the near future.

For now, never again raise your voice in anger or impatience, ever. Then things concerning bitches and bitch-boys will begin to become apparent in your increasing cold and calculating mind's eye.

» Add a comment «

Sam J.   May 2, 2016 12:59 PM EDT

I read Rat Ratification and got a good chuckle and a bit horror. Nice story.

Sean   May 1, 2016 12:43 PM EDT

A prerequisite for a woman? Wow. Ever since I became an adult and left my constantly screaming mother behind I vowed to ditch any woman that yelled and have happily linked myself a non yelling female. I have however noticed I raise my voice far too much to get my point across. Looking forward this series.

Sam J.   May 1, 2016 11:42 AM EDT

Ran across this article on abandoned houses in Baltimore.

https://www.washingtonpost.com/local/baltimo

re-has-more-than-16000-vacant-houses-why-cant-the-homeless-move-in/2015/05/12/3fd6b068-f7ed-11e4-9030-b4732caefe81_story.html

Choice quotes,"... 46,800 vacant homes — 16 percent of Baltimore's housing stock..."

"All of Baltimore's social, economic and political issues are encapsulated by the vacant houses...They're vacant because of economic and political forces." said Jeff Singer

I say they're vacant because hood rats live there.

"...vacant buildings are associated with numerous problems. One recent study showed that abandoned buildings are associated with higher rates of "assaultive violence." Another found that residents who live near vacant building have a far greater chance of falling victim to fires..."

I think the government has misinformed us. We have been lied to. It's not guns that kill people. it's vacant buildings!!! I've found the answer! Rejoice and jubilate at my genius. All we have to do now is do something about those vacant houses and all will be good.

"...[Why couldn't $130 million transform one of Baltimore's poorest places?]...:

And why wouldn't we build condos on Mt. St. Helens?

JL responds: May 2, 2016 8:53 AM EDT

Thanks for the links, Sam J.

Check out my article title Rat Ratification, about my interviews with Baltimore housing inspectors. They told me at the time that there were 25,000 vacancies [this was in 2001] and that the City had two vans with two men each for boarding up and reboarding vacants that had been raided for copper, with each team able to board two houses per day! Do the math, bro!

Who Gets Loud and Why?

On Running Bitches and Bitch-Boys: Part 1

Who are the loudest people?

The people with the least self control are the loudest.

My Grandmother Kern, descended from the Irish slave side of the family, used to cuss a blue-streak at my grandfather. Her favorite saying was, "Goddamn it, Fred!"

He, my German grandfather, would say "Oh, Mary, relax."

To which she would say, "Goddamn it, you relax, Fred!"

To which he would answer, "I am relaxing." Then he would smile slightly, wait for her to finish fussing and then kindly tell her how it was going to be. When he died she was a terrible sight to see, a formerly "strong" person now weak, for her strength was gone.

I have always attempted to emulate the quiet elders in my family, like my other grandmother, who was easily twice as smart as her in-law, the one descended from the Canadian white slaves, quiet as a mouse and sharp as a tack.

As a youth, I noticed that the strong men: the boxing coaches, wrestling coaches, the smart football coaches, and the strongest men in the family, would make you listen through force of will, with patience, by waiting for you to stop and then making you listen closely by not speaking too loudly. The pussies, though, the wannabe gym teachers and third rate high school football coaches, they all yelled.

My mother yelled when she couldn't get her way. I knew that for a woman, yelling was one step away from tearful meltdown or crazed explosion, both easily managed behavioral progressions in which the observer has a clearer tactical view than the actor.

The frightened white kids I rode the bus with yelled when we went through the black neighborhood, terrified yet emboldened by their high armored vantage point. I, the silent one, was the only one on the bus with the courage to walk through that same black neighborhood and they left me alone because I was quiet, quiet like the strong men that were still present in over half of black families, not loud like their babbling mammas, but silent like sentinels—how things have changed.

Why Do People Get Loud?

1. Those who feel unappreciated and unnoticed, who lack confidence and a centered being, make noise to draw attention to themselves, attention that their presence and deeds fail to earn.

2. Stupid people, who lack a vocabulary adequate to express their thoughts, will raise their voice when unable to impress others with their simple opinion.

3. Those who lack serenity, peace-of-mind, discipline, self-control, who lack the entire spectrum of warrior qualities necessary for the toilsome task of becoming skilled in combat. Those who lack the above qualities

tend to demonstrate their failings through over verbalization and dependence on redundant verbal bonding [rap and hiphop, for instance] signaling to any warrior within earshot that they might be easily taken, especially once isolated from their support group. For example, the most respected fighter in Ancient Greece, was not a general, a king, or even the best at his warrior art, but a moral force. He was a champion boxer who single-handedly destroyed a slavery-ring masquerading as a religious cult. He was named Gracespeaker not Loudgrunter.

4. Women are more vocal than men for this very reason, that they are weak and powerless in real situations and must therefore be able to call for aid, plead for mercy and scream as they die so the other women can scatter and bring the men.

5. People representing a social power structure that is more powerful than they, that is more powerful than those they are charged with leading, directing, managing, torturing, etc., may effectively use increased vocal volume as a necessity in noisy situations and as a compliance amplifier. This is in imitation of the

lion's roar, which startles the puny primate so that he will freeze and be easily torn apart. There is then, the fact that women, children and weaklings may be startled by masters and other aggressors via the use of the tactical shout, verbal raging, etc.

In the following installment we will begin with a legitimate uses of the tactical shout.

In the meantime, if you are interested in the concept, checkout my book Of Lions and Men.

» Add a comment «

Bernie Hackett   May 3, 2016 8:12 PM EDT

It's what we used to call "Getting their attention".

To be used sparingly.

It isn't effective if that's all you have, 'cause it becomes old real fast.

I always figured the loudest of folks were secretly frightened, and out of their depth. Of course, given that situation, I'd shut the hell up, but that's just me.

I like compliance amplifier.

Rolling Over like the Great Khan

Ted Has a Man Question for the Maniacal Misogynist On Bitches

"James, if it's not bad enough to have the same name as a creepy stuffed animal that cusses out Mark Wahlberg in bad movies I have found myself short of female companionship as a general rule of the nerdish existence. I'm not some weirded out caveman like you or some black thug so women don't exactly flock my way. But—through becoming a more interesting guy and not trying to push my opinion on people I have not only learned more from the human debris with which I am consigned to spend 48 hours a week of my miserable life but have become interesting to women. So, this has resulted in me having sex with someone other than my hand which has really gotten complicated. I have a question for you and you seem arrogant enough to address it honestly. If you answer this in such a way that it helps me maintain a hold on this wet crevice I stumbled into I pledge to buy a copy of Your Trojan Whorse which I have niggardly been reading online.

"Okay, it amazed me that I didn't cum right away—and amazed her too, because she's been around and I haven't. Well, eventually, it happened. Then I fell asleep and she is chattering in an insecure fashion saying, "Now that you got my pussy you don't want any more conversation. You're just like the rest—just blow your load and roll over. Is there something the matter with me?"

Stop Right There!
Ted, I have deleted your page of recriminating commentary, self-loathing analysis and vaginal worship, because, frankly it's embarrassing. But more importantly, because the only thing that matters right here is what your bitch said—because, you know, it's all about her.

Really, every word that comes out of your mouth in her presence must either ignore her and her sensibilities unapologetically or be sculpted for her consumption. You cannot engage in information exchange with a woman—not even your mother—without either being an asshole or a master manipulator. Conversations with women can go wrong at any moment, so resist the temptation to say too much in regard to her attention to your obviously adequate body. You see, this dumb bitch thinks she is attached to your nerd mind, when in fact she just stumbled upon some porno cock dressed up like a collectable card geek. Women cannot think on their feet, their knees or their back.

You see, she is in crisis. This is what went off in her mind when she actually experienced good dick for the first time in her life. Keep in mind that as few men can fuck well as can fight well. It is a small club, and if your narrow-assed, dweebish self has managed to morph into Jake Steed in the confines of her ill-appointed bedroom she has just said to herself something like:

Disclaimer: This is a look inside the tangled confines of the American female mind. You might not emerge sane after reading it.

"All of those retarded black guys and fat white rednecks I blew to find a nice dick, and here it is—fucking like a porn star and looking like the revenge of the nerds—I can't let him know—oh, shit, I screamed when I had the triple-O—this fucking geek knows he's the bomb and will be lining up black rap dancers in a week and will have forgotten all about Little Old Me, who just wanted to be able to cum without the hand nozzle attachment on the kitchen sink...what the fuck, I've got to get him on the defensive. He lacks confidence, or he wouldn't have had sex with the chick who blew the football team—They ought to outlaw Gatorade, that shit tasted like bleach—so it won't be hard to beat him back down—but I like it when he treats me like a sexual conquest, and this motherfucker could actually make some money, maybe buy me a house and if I beat him down too far he might start fucking Asian stick-figured bitches to feel powerful and, Oh, Aunt Jane, why did you have to have a stroke right when I needed your advice on men..."

Okay, Ted, the above thought pattern is why we don't let bitches negotiate with Iran over nuclear armament!

Fortunately, all you need to do is concentrate on the little bit she said, because the mess in her head is far beyond repair in any case and the best you can do is earn your peace and quiet.

So, if I'm laying there after dropping a load on a bitch that says, "Now that you got my pussy you don't want any more conversation. You're just like the rest—just blow your load and roll over. Is there something the matter with me?"

I would and have, typically—listen up, Bro—roll over like a predator fetus and growl under my breath.

I guarantee you that this will get her to repeat the last line, "Is there something the matter with me?" which is really all bitches think about. So, you have to accomplish two things with your response, (1) get her to accept the fact that she is a bitch and (2) convince her that you, uniquely, have no idea how fucked up in the head she is and that you think she is just fine the way she is [Hello, because she's sucking your dick she is, by definition, just fine the way she is], and that she is therefore not just any bitch, but your bitch.

Ted, here it goes, the fewer words the better. As she peeks over your shoulder, trying to examine your face for any sign of insincerity and repeats, "Is there something the matter with me?" you snarl slightly in irritation and say, "Bitch, nah!"

You then try to get some more sleep, to which she will—relieved that you don't know about her sucking off all 64 members of your university football team—say, "But you're normally so talkative, so intelligent, and now you just want to curl up and sleep and I'm all energized and want to plant flowers, and clean the house—"

You now cut her off with the karate-pimp-hand chop-wave and intone, sagaciously, bringing out the nerd when you need him, "These are both chemical responses to the consummated rape and insemination of the female human by her conqueror, who, having slain her menfolk, is now prevented by the hand of Nature from slaughtering her children, as lions do. If you're feeling energetic, go cook me dinner or blow me. I'll eventually wake up."

Ted, this really works, sets the wench back on her heels, and results in human symbiosis. Back around 2004, while in my savage prime, I once used this exact same line on two chicks in the same week, who were both regulars. Mrs. Bedwrecker was so thrilled about the final suggestion that she just started having my roommate [a lady who liked ladies] let her in and she would have sex with me while I was asleep. Now, that is a symbiotic relationship and totally cut out the need to discuss draperies, purse fashion and eye-liner on my part. The other chick, though, Tannika Rita, would have actually fit into the primitive barbarian setting I was evoking in my Genghis Khan-like boast, to which she snarled playfully over my shoulder as she tugged on my chest hair, "Yeah, Mother Nature puts you bastards to sleep after you use us so just in case the dick wasn't good, we can slit your throat!"

I never fell asleep under Tannika Rita again, just in case she had a sudden rise in expectations.

Ted, it worked for me, so it can work for you.

» Add a comment «
Hank   May 19, 2016 1:14 PM EDT

Don't ever change, man.

David   May 13, 2016 12:22 PM EDT

Wait, you mean we can't let women negotiate on issues of national security? WTF, LOL.

Great article in all its Neanderthal glory.

David

'Hey!'

The Only Latino in a Black Bar: On Running Bitches and Bitch-Boys: Part 2

Raphael has ever been a sucker for fine pussy, and as he gets older, nearing sixty, that fine pussy is multiplying, because his eyesight is failing, and those lovelies are getting younger...

Raphael had just sworn off of women a few months ago. Then, two weeks back, he starts speaking to me about this fine young mixed race Latina-ChiNegroi baby doll who asked him to come see her at the bar where she works in Western Baltimore County, out in Owings Mills, a supposedly civilized setting...

Despite his pledge to the he-man woman-haters club and our vow to set an example for the young knuckleheads under our care, when the vertical eye winked and those designer claws beckoned, he walked wide-eyed into the den of the tigress...

Raphael was a lightweight kick-boxer in another century. Now he's a dude looking at knee-replacement surgery who neglected to bring his knife and finds himself in bar packed with about 50 black men, ranging from age 30-50, which puts him on the old side. From his years working barroom doors he noticed this was a problem spot by the posture of the bouncer out front, but was not impressed with the job the bouncer did on keeping an eye on the hot barmaid, which is the main asset when you are drawing clientele that grew up dreaming about the being the brother on the Hennessey billboard with a fine Asian chick on one arm and a light-skinned mulattress on the other arm.

Raphael is the guy pictured on the cover of the book in this link:

https://www.amazon.com/Logic-Steel-Fighters-Blade-Encountersebook/dp/B004WRHQHW?ie=UTF8&keywords=james%20lafond&qid=1463260869&ref_=sr_1_10&s=books&sr=1-10

The lady had saved a seat for him at the bar opposite her register. [I later explained to him that she was seducing him to provide auxiliary security.]

As he takes his first free drink a muscular 30-year-old black man steps behind the bar, steps up to her and begins screaming at her and threatening to hurt her for watering his drinks, which obviously was untrue as evidenced by his extreme inebriation.

Raphael looks around the bar and just sees the black dudes watching, none of them willing to step up and defend the girl they all want to take home, sure evidence that he is in the suburbs with "Oreo-niggas" as my friend Calvin Wiley would have called them, black dudes with the coward heart of a white man. If this had happened at the mixed-race sports bar I frequent there would have been a contest between the black guys at the back of the bar and the white guys at the front of the bar to see who got their hands on the loudmouth first. But, this is the suburbs, and only one set of gonads showed up.

Raphael leaned over the bar, and used the same loud voice he uses to yell instructions to fighters in a crowded arena, and roared, "Hey!!"

This caused everyone in the bar to become silent and turn and look at him, and for the bitch-boy to begin measuring his youth and size against the older man. Twenty years ago, Raphael would have [and did] ended up in jail after doing some ridiculous martial arts overkill on this guy in front of his friends. But, decades wiser, he smiled, raised his finger, pointed it down at the man delicately, and looked to the front door where the huge bouncer had been greeting a friend, and whispered, "Security."

The bitch boy was soon in the gargantuan grasp of the bouncer, who was also a cop and held the punk until an on-duty officer got there to cuff him and charge him with assault, and Raphael savored the victory of age and wisdom over anger and youth. The young lady kept buying his drinks and he was gentleman enough not to discuss the rest of the evening.

This is an excellent example of the effective use of volume in limiting violence. After the first shout, action or contrastingly level words, as required by the situation, will be more effective that maintaining the loud tone. You have now drawn attention to yourself and should be keyed up for action and aware of threats and options. Continued yelling will tend to be counterproductive.

'The Mulattress is a Queenmaker'

The Mayor that Roasted Marshmallow Cops as Her City Burned is Backing the Wicked Witch of the Left in Her Bid for Autarch

Thank you, my secret agent in the U.K., for the link and that snappy quote.

I find it fascinating that we are no living subject to a plot that could have formed the basis of a Conan story. On a personal level, the fact that I put forward Stephanie Rawlings-Blake as the mayor I would most want to have sex with, in a heated discussion with my friend Quinn, who insisted that former Harm City executive Steala Dixon would make for a better tryst, I feel betrayed! After sitting there in front of white nationalist, Mescaline

Franklin, defending this woman's goddess precinct, even after Quinn described her eating an entire bucket of fried chicken during a City Council meeting he attended, only to have her turn around and put forth a candidate for Queen of the World that is not even fuckable by the most antiquitous Pictish standards simply puts me beyond words!

However, I now better understand how the Mulattress mayor shall be rewarded for her cupidity masquerading as stupidity. It's not going to be Gloriana, but then again, I don't think you could pay Michael Moorcock enough to write this script.

http://www.dailymail.co.uk/news/article-3273404/Democratic-National-Committeewoman-says-party-clearing-path-Hillary-women-charge-want-way.html

'Disarm the Cops'

And Give Convicted Felons the Right to Vote: The New Solution to Black Crime by Robert Weissberg

Thanks to my anonymous sleuth for uncovering these crumbling bricks beneath the Dyke of Ages.

First, as an honorary African American, I take umbrage at the suggestion that there is such a thing as "black crime." Taxing privilege and recovering damages in the form of reparations should never be construed as crime. I am beings serious here. All of these sissy white people that believe the government should protect them from criminals should be heaped into the same mass grave as the left wingers who desperately want to be robbed and raped to assuage the terrible guilt they feel for being born without a purpose.

Check out the metro-sexual creature holding the "Disarm the Cops" sign and try and justify his existence. Any race that produces men like this and fails to castrate them and put them to work waxing my concubine's stupendous buttocks should be crushed under Fate's heavy tread.

http://www.unz.com/article/the-new-solution-to-black-crime/

» Add a comment «
Glasgow Ned May 15, 2016 10:25 AM EDT

That last paragraph is literary gold!

Caught in The Pecking Order

Henhouse Behavior at the Workplace by Lili Hun

Treatment of women by women is often different from how women may treat men. Women often suck up to men while treating their female coworkers quite negatively.

What I would like to query is who controls henhouse and how do they do it?

To begin, let's explore overt vs. covert control.

Overt may consist of a raised voice, public reprimanding or ridicule, demeaning or cutting comments.

Under this heading of mostly verbal behaviors, a topic that deserves attention of its own is how the hen treats those who come to her for help. She may lash out at a person when they come for help, punishing the person for requesting it. She may say that she told you something already, even if it was months ago and only once. You then avoid asking questions or showing ignorance, which will negatively affect your function and effectiveness, so you're damned if you do and damned if you don't.

It's a particular problem when a rooster tells you to ask the hen questions and the top hen reacts unpleasantly, thereby making you the problem for coming to her. She is likely to try to make you feel stupid. If you have an analytical head on your shoulders and are capable of explaining the matter to her specifically, you will still be digging your own grave, because that will be interpreted as insubordination, rather than trying to clean the shit she has put in your path from your boots. I'm also going to say that this is more likely to happen if you are intelligent and therefore perceived as a threat, especially if your vocabulary and sentence complexity are not at the level of an average newspaper article.

Covert control may include exclusion, avoidance including conversation or invitations, and only greeting if spoken to first.

Withholding critical information that you need to function in your environment is great for a game of cat and mouse. This includes a calculated way of giving information necessary to do the job by withholding some important detail. Inadequate training and no standard operating procedures or software manuals can compound the problems of learning in a henhouse, which will become your learning deficiency and may not be accidental. She may avoid giving you the forest overview and release one tree of information at a time. I would also posit that learning isn't well understood, and teaching is often done badly. If your workplace is understaffed, your questions also become a hindrance to those same hens who are struggling to do their double workload.

If there is an attempt to discuss this with the rooster, she will deny her behavior or reframe it to something less damning in conversation with him. If it's about you, negative assumptions and interpretations will abound. Blaming those supervised by the top hens is a given, regardless of whether it's rightfully assigned. Her agenda is to keep her place in the pecking order, and to this end, she will put stumbling blocks in your way to waste your energy and hasten failure. She will be most successful at keeping the rooster hoodwinked if he is not a rooster but a capon in disguise.

If you're a woman reading this, think back to the 7th and 8th grade social environment for a snapshot of negative female behaviors and coping with the superficial social structure. It's still the same in a henhouse with adult hen women. When I've observed them in action, I don't understand how they have the emotional energy to create drama and make misery for others. Honestly, I've always had far fewer friendships with women, because it's just easier for me to avoid these behaviors. I've had little success working with them.

If you're a man reading this, I'd be interested in any henhouse observations you may want to share with me, as a relative outsider.

On the lighter side, while driving into the countryside, I saw a "Free Manure" sign on the side of the road, and I reflected on how generously these hens dispense manure to those around them, wanted or not.

Lili Hun

As the former rooster in a 75-hen hen house this seems to my crowing vantage to be an accurate bottom view of the same work environment that drove me crazy from the top end, even though I had the ability to effect change. I eventually resigned and enjoy poverty far more than having a full wallet and lording it over this viciously clucking multitude. On a lighter note, once when in a pet store, looking for a small animal for my son, I saw two female parakeets pecking a male parakeet viciously in the head and our decision was made. Captain lived bitch-free for ten years.

The Bitch that Laid Your Egg

Nigel's Cautionary Tale

Overall, the message of On Bitches, is the fact that a man may not hope to productively engage in discussion with women and those neutered males who have been hatched from the eggs laid by the queens of non-fathered households. If you are the son of such a bitch as described in this brief account, you must distance yourself from the one that has as her goal your emasculation as a way of expressing her bitterness against your absentee father.

Nigel's mother looked like a professional prize-fighter, so may have been correct in blaming the absence of her mate on his choice. In any case, she struts the earth with a mean attitude. At about age 10, Nigel and Benson were playing video games in the basement when mama walked down stairs, cursing like a sailor and accusing Nigel of making a mess in the living room upstairs. Nigel began to explain the mess and his mother, easily twice his size and known to fight men in the middle of the street, balled up her fist and punched him in the eye.

He then finished saying, "It was your boyfriend that made that mess in the living room."

As his eye swelled up, she stalked of up the stairs without even an apology. To this day she speaks to him in the cruelest fashion, calling him names and drawing attention to his weak sense of masculine identity, which she herself scrubbed from his being before it could form.

As one might imagine, arguing with Nigel or his mother could not be a profitable exercise, especially in stressful circumstances.

Do not engage verbally with bitches or their spawn and expect anything other than emotive escalation.

Smart Bitches

How to Manage the Functional Intelligence of Friends, Foes, Felons and Females

Like it or not, we live in a world of bitches, in which the constant search for the moral holy grail of victim status by most of America makes "Bitchdom" the real matrix, with the United States of Whatever this was Supposed to Be residing firmly in the land of fantasy and fable.

The purpose of a bitch is to provide a master with a slave. For instance, the lowly worker who gripes and complains or "bitches" all of the time about his cruel boss, is actually maintaining his own enslavement and serving his master by letting off emotional pressure. In this way he shall continue to serve and scrape and bitch and moan rather than going postal and whacking his boss or setting up his own business and challenging his former employer.

In my four years as the general manger of a 110-person workplace, I discovered that the most important facet of my job was winnowing the bitch-chaff from the brain. Very few people have functional workplace brains, and either mindlessly comply or complain, or, as is usually the case, engage in both alternately. Most employees cannot function as decision makers in the workplace because they have zero imagination, no way in which to see the situation from the perspective of the customer or the owner, both of which perspectives have to be constantly juggled by any retail food manger. I found who had brains—in other words, who was not the victimhood-questing bitch—and set them up as managers or as independent laborers answerable to me for the completion of their special details, depending on their mentality.

I have only worked with a limited pool of bitches [about 600 total, over 30 years] and have found no such creature among Asians or

Latinos, only among Palefaces and Darkhides. What I am discussing here is how the rare masculine person can dominate the massive, emasculated Body Catatonic that is postmodern America. The advice is simple, indicating what makes these people far less able to act intelligently.

White Males

The white male is the butt of every joke, fear and hatred used by society to prevent him from ascending within himself or to the top of the crumbling social order. He is either an actor, a man with agency, a wolf, or he behaves as one of the types of moral chattel below, in which case he gets what he deserves.

Black Males, Adult

The presence of every additional black man draws down the intelligence of all the black men in the group by roughly 10%. By the time you have ten black men together you basically have an intoxicated or agitated colony of sperm. Israel Flood, an old sharecropper I once worked with had a favorite saying, "How stupid can one black man be?" which he used to draw attention to particularly stupid black men.

When drawing down black male intelligence by grouping them together, be careful not to make too large a group. This is the reason why basketball squads are limited to five players on the court. With 20 dudes on the court it would just be a fight.

The presence of even one sympathetic white man [You, cracker, yes you!] who is not an emasculated liberal or rabble rouser [the guy in the suit on the sidelines], will nullify much of this effect and may even channel the group energy to good use.

Black Males, Youth

Oppressed youth share the characteristics of Black Male, Adults [who they fail to become in large numbers] and the bitch queen welfare incubators that "father" them. It falls to the actor to determine whether or not the youth in question is acting as a bitch or an adult male, for there is no male childhood to speak of in this community, but either a state of perpetual emasculation or a frantic attempt to claim some conceptualized ideal of manhood from the ruins of a fatherless beginning.

White Women

The insertion of a penis in a white woman cuts her intelligence immediately in half. Orgasms each draw down the aggregate intellect by 10%. If you are any kind of man you have had a Paleface babe say something like, "No, I don't know what the checking account balance is—you just fucked me stupid, you callous prick!"

I have found that tasks appropriate to restoring the operative intelligence of your mate or plaything—that is, if such is a desirable use of her potential—include:

1. Fetching the coldest beer from the cooler. Be a nice guy and let her have a taste before sending her back for the next.

2. Giving you a massage.

3. Reading a passage from one of John Norman's Gor novels.

4. Cleaning your room.

5. If she can handle that, let her order a pizza.

Black Women

Okay, black women are immune to dick-induced stupidity. They have all been raped at such a young age that they essentially behave as if they have just been inseminated 24-hours a day. Recall how, after fucking your white bitch stupid, you let her work up to the complex task of ordering pizza?

Yes, then, so you don't just roll out of bed and have your black bitch order a pizza, because she will cuss out the Pakistani chick over the phone and you'll end up with rat shit and nominally-Islamic saliva for toppings. You must avoid letting your black bitch verbalize. If she is going to order a pizza, then bend her over and give her the phone, because she can only talk sense or remain calm while subject to intercourse. Although she will be coherent and relatively sedate, expect a lot of repetition.

Okay, I have a supporting story.

Mom, stop reading.

Son, listen up and learn.

When I lived with Ajay from 2003-10, this girl named Tina used to visit me. She was pretty, as dark as my jump boots and had that lithe build that Robert E. Howard forever waxed sub-philosophical about. Black chicks with their own hair paste it with grease, so you have to borrow your roommate's centennial place mat to put on your pillow. When you put it back on the table she'll think she just spilled some salad dressing...

Everything went great on the "let's get to know each other while you practice for your clarinet recital" second date. But, a half hour into the third date, all of that instrumentation got her bothered and—suffice it to say, that for the roughly ninety minutes that I reenacted the Conquest of Dahomey by The Legion Estranger she said the same three words over and over and over and over again, until I realized, that I was going to be knee deep in cheese pizzas if I let her place the order.

In any case, there is no way you can get your black bitch to order a pizza, because, undicked, they will get in an argument, and dicked, they will order a dozen.

Okay, we kind of got off track here, but if you live around the corner from a good pizza joint it was not a wasted trip into my sordid past.

The point is, engaging a black bitch in conversation has the same effect as jamming a white bitch's IUD into her spine—it makes her stupid, immediately and this is a problem because black bitches are more violent then Salvadoran bank robbers. For this reason, there are only three ways to communicate with a black bitch:

1. Argue pointlessly until she hits you, which, if you are a cop and you need an arrest to get that dickhead merit badge, could be useful.

2. Strike the benign White Daddy pose. Nod as if concerned with her wretched plight. Sigh sympathetically when her voice raises [this will cause her to lower her voice so she can hear the sympathetic sigh]. When she catchers her breath do not say "I understand," because, as stupid as she is, she knows you don't understand, but say, "How can I help you?" This takes a while but will eventually result in her needing a hug or a handshake and will end sometime within an hour.

3. The following method does not work with black bitches and youth who are anatomically male, only with authentic queens. Wax sympathetic as explained above, while you are

blatantly checking her out. Look at her body and her face as if you cannot help yourself. This even works, and works better, if she is not attractive! Where an ugly white chick would think you were playing her or you were blind and would screw anything, God gave black chicks the magic ability to look in the mirror and see Miss Universe. I say, if the Man Above puts a tool in your hand then use it!

Okay, Son, keep your bitch boys at a distance, your bitches close and all of them stupid.

» Add a comment «

Fatmanjudo May 27, 2016 11:02 PM EDT

I heard a good expression to describe the phenomena you describe as "dick drunk". Also another good insight concerning when they come home and tell you all their problems and you start to go into rational problem solving mode-don't bother. They don't want you to solve their problem they want you to solve their mood.

'Not as Mature as You Thought'

Dealing with the Rage of Bitch-Boys, for Intact Black Men

Last night, as I walked down the backstreets of Hamilton to Northern Parkway, I noticed Tiny Dancer, a girl whose family lives in a house at my favorite bus stop. She looks like a gymnast, tiny in her jeans and wife-beater, with short-cropped hair. I inadvertently frightened her and her girlfriend—a Frank Frazzetta chick that looked like she jumped off the cover of a Conan comic—and their large, sweet potato-shaped cock-blocker, who squealed girlishly when I passed them on the sidewalk.

I silently wished Tiny Dancer well on her little dyke date and awaited the bus, which actually seemed to be looking for me. I suppose the driver is getting lonely, with a mere 8 souls on the last bus of the night that used to carry 28.

Having foolishly committed myself to sitting on the back deck—essentially an act of suicidal self-loathing for giving up fighting, which is the only thing that ever made me feel vital—that will eventually result in a nasty fight with the worst elements that flock back there. I noticed that the patrons were all in their 30s and returning from work—not a thug in sight. It must have been prom night in the ghetto. On the bus rolled without its obligatory handful of criminals.

The phone in my pocket vibrated and I saw that it was Oliver, normally neck deep in some desperate divorcee by this time on Friday night, so, hoping all was well in Oliverland, I answered.

Oliver: How are you doing, James?

James: Currently, the only labrat on the hoodrat conveyance. I'll be at the gym on Sunday, but won't be sparring. I was in a car accident on I-95 yesterday and have some torn intercostals, maybe a compressed cartilage. Wearing the backpack tonight was not a good idea. How about you?

Oliver: James, do you ever get the feeling that you're not as mature as you thought you were?

James: Yeah, like three minutes ago. It's a daily occurrence at this point. So, the beard isn't growing in well?

Laughter

Oliver: James, today I was driving a client, a really good guy who I have done a lot of work for. He was in the backseat as we are headed across Northern Parkway to Falls Road. Then the car in front pulls up short, so I have to stop and the guy behind me bumps the curb and was really pissed about it and started shouting. I just kept my eyes forward, even when he pulls up alongside me and starts telling me to pull over, calling me a bitch, telling me he's going to kick my ass. I didn't respond, just kept driving...and he would not let up, just kept at it.

James: So he was an Asian guy?

Oliver: No.

James: A Jewish dude?

Oliver: No.

James: You're kidding me. You mean we still have regular white-boys over there on the West Side picking fights with a hard working brother?

Oliver: He wasn't white, James. You know who he was.

James: Okay, please tell me you didn't drop him on his head.

Oliver: I just don't get how these guys can be so confident.

James: It's the low IQ.

Oliver: So he could have gone at the light, but stays there in front of me so he can continue this shit. Finally, I cracked the door just to let him know I wasn't backing down. You know how some people believe God tests you like this? Well, I believe in karma, and think that maybe God put me there to shut this guy up. Then my client notices the door is cracked and says something about this being a scary situation, so I closed it, and then the guy really pops off with calling me a bitch and telling me he's going to come over there and snatch me out of my car, so I look back ahead. You know, I really wanted to snatch this guy up and lay him out. But I'm glad I didn't. Not only would I have lost this client but a State Trooper rolled by like a minute later

James: You have to realize that some yo on the street is going to go down within seconds. In 20 seconds you're probably dragging this guy's body onto the median, and that is about when witnesses start to see stuff. Never respond to a challenge, you'll look like the aggressor almost immediately. Cameras come out and there you are, looking like a child abuser on the side of the road. Only put them down if they touch you.

Oliver: But why me, why did he select me? I don't have much of an ego left. I don't even knock guys out that I know can't take it while they're beating my ass sparring. I just don't want to give ground like that. I don't grill people or anything.

[Actually, Oliver has a very kind, open face. One would never guess he was a fighter to look into his face unless you've been in boxing gyms and recognize the sleepy look.]

James: The client, was he white?

Oliver: Yes, an older dude in his mid-forties.

James: The punk didn't look at or threaten the client did he? Would he have gone after this client if he were by himself?

Oliver: Hell no!

James: He was counting on the white man talking you out of fighting, so had a pretty clear shot at punking you out. You aren't used to this because black chicks like to see their men fight. But when you're with most white women, punks will come out of the woodwork to make threats they won't have to backup, because they know your bitch will not support you. If Fred Sanford [the cantankerous junkyard operator played on TV by black comedian Red Foxx circa 1980] was in the back seat, do you think this punk would have called you out?

Oliver: No, not at all.

James: The important thing is you didn't take the bait. In a just world he dies on his knees. But we live in a corrupt society and have to be able to deal with The State's preference for evil.

Oliver: Thanks, James. You know there is another edition of Hidden Colors coming out in theaters.

James: Cool, how about if I take a bucket of Kentucky fried chicken to the theatre?

Oliver: How about if you watch it with Erique and me at my place over a few drinks?

James: Sure.

Oliver: Be safe, James.

James: See you on Sunday, Bro.

One other person offloaded with me, and was met by her escort—few people in Essex walking alone at night anymore—as other bus patrons waited for cabs or hacks. I saw the first County Cop cruising on Old Eastern Avenue in 13 months. He pulled over a motorist who was not speeding, presumably for some other violation, 100 feet short of two young thugs who were exchanging something under the waving branches of the night-shrouded trees on the sidewalk across from the crab house, right in his headlights.

I suppose the lesson of the night is that a man must pick his battles.

Owning the Bitch-Raised Boy

Management of Rage When Dealing with the Moral Chattel of the Mammy State: On Running Bitches And Bitch-Boys: Part 3

The following is the method I developed for calming down irate men while working as the general manager of a Baltimore City supermarket and also as the head of security for a handful of collectable card events in the Washington D.C. area, both venues that were dominated by violent crime and aggressive behavior on the part of large, young, black men.

This also works with loud white men as well. With the whites you can get a better resolution because they usually respond well to smooth, low tones of voice imploring them to behave reasonably for their own self-interest. Do not try this with blacks as over 95% of black men and youth were abandoned by their father and abused by their mother, at some time and at some level, and they therefore behave like giant toddlers with the vocabulary of a welfare mother, whenever the unjust actions of white people have caused their anger to rise.

Understand

-When angry they have zero capacity for reason.

-If in the company of any other person who is not a white man they will resist being brought to reason, because...

-Their anger is sacred, the one thing in the world that respects the whimpering infant within who was slapped and screamed at in his cradle, in his stroller, in his high chair, in his car seat, and then kicked and punched and beaten as a toddler as he ambled about a cruel, uncaring world. His pain is immense and he will commit any outrageous act to vent it so long as he feels...

-A sense of justification, if only momentary, will enable him to act out violently and become deified as the Nat Turner of his own sorry drama, which no one will even watch unless he "does some really dumb shit."

-He needs to have aggression, resistance to his aggression, or disapproval of his aggression—even understanding will do the trick [so don't say "I understand" because you can't], so do not feed his aggression with any of the following.

If you are being called to deal with this person detail an employee to call the police. In many cases him overhearing this will put him into pleading injustice mode rather than threat mode. But don't be rude about it. Don't let him think you wanted him to know the cops were coming. You must project confidence that you can deal with anything. Remember, he never had a daddy. Although he might hate to admit it, he'd give almost anything for a real daddy—even a white devil daddy like you.

Aggression Feeds

1. Do not speak to him.

2. Do not glare or otherwise make eye-contact with him.

3. Do not touch him.

4. Do not extend your hand towards him.

5. Do not step up to him.

6. Do not stand square with him.

7. Do not step back away from him.

8. Do not look away from him.

9. Do not walk away from him.

10. Do not challenge or disrespect his sacred, emasculated rage in any way, for it is the acid vat in which his resolve shall dissolve if he is left to soak in it.

11. Do not make eye contact but watch his chin and chest, which will permit you to notice the movement of his elbows. If you have stood at the proper distance he will not be able to touch you without moving his elbow.

Aggression Drains

1. Stand slightly off to his side, with your lead foot to the outside of his nearest foot.

2. If possible, step to the outside of his left foot with your right foot and then heel pivot so that you left foot and shoulder are behind and in line with your right side.

3. Slowly raise your rear left hand so that your wrist touches your nipple and your hand is open toward him, over your shoulder, in front of your neck. You have just denied two kills targets incase he breaks out a knife and you're slower than him.

4. Your lead right hand should be one hand higher than his lead left hand and extended slightly, very slightly. If his hand is by his side, yours is by his belt. Etc.

5. Both of your hands are deployed defensively and are open.

6. Tuck your chin.

7. He will feel the need to maintain chest to chest or shoulder alignment confrontation with you and will step around with his rear foot. When he does so this takes emotional effort

on his part and you step around to maintain your defensive, oblique orientation. Every time he steps around this requires him to recharge his anger and will dump the adrenaline that will poison him.

8. If he tries to touch you with either hand or both, slightly raise and extend the open hand detailed to that zone and draw off, doing a slight drag step that takes you diagonally away from his body, and places his lead foot between his rear foot and you, which will prevent him from striking hard with his rear hand.

9. Once you have extended a hand or hands in response to his crowding you [but have drawn off to avoid having to resist with your hands] do not lower that hand or hands. If you do, he may strike.

10. When he pleads with you to argue, to fight, shrug your shoulder and tilt your head gently, as if you are stupid.

11. If he looks down to his right he's going to sucker punch you with that hand as he looks back up. In response to him looking down, step

off again, behind his lead foot and he will have to reset.

12. If this backs you against a wall, slide along it.

13. If your continual step around is blocked by an obstacle, duck slightly behind your open hands as you step off to his other side and employ the mirror image gambit from there.

14. If he attacks, defend yourself with your extended open hands as you step around and draw off.

What Usually Happens

1. Such men usually begin to worry that the calm responder is calm because he is assured that the police will side with him, or that the responder is some kind of psycho, and the only thing that scares blacks into a surely silence is "A stone cold white muthafaca" "who is crazy too."

2. Wolfers, or noisily threatening men of any type, are either permanently or temporarily emasculated. If this is a guy you know, just talk him off subject as you get between him

and his target and save him some embarrassment. If you are not someone who he trusts and respects, a black man will not let you talk him down and you must instead adopt the role of tiring, oblique target of his rage. This is a woman with a penis and he will have the same need as a woman to escalate his anger through adversarial verbalization in order to build courage for an attack on you and also to build resolve among his companions. His companions draw closer to his cause with every word you say, and draw more unsure of his course with every considered silence that meets one of his raging statements.

3. Raging is tiring business and he will usually drift away, in stages, stepping back at you repeatedly to make a threat or lodge an accusation. However, his steps away will be longer then his steps back to you. This is generally a face-saving tactic.

4. Their lack of intelligence and extremely limited vocabulary—which ironically often leads to such outbursts—will often solve the problem, as they repeat the same rageful sayings over and over again, eventually calming themselves. All it takes from you is one word

to wipe their frail memory of shouting threats clean and they will amp back up and rage with renewed fury. You wouldn't speak during a funeral service, would you? Well, this is the funeral of his masculinity—whatever shreds he might have held on to. Have some respect, you white devil.

5. On some occasions raging urban justice heroes will begin to hyperventilate, rub their head in an attempt not to cry, wring their hands in frustration as they prance, hang their head in shame or in brooding insolence, lose their voice, and even break down in tears, which will usually result in them turning away in shame. This can happen within a minute, usually two, and few bitch-raised boys are able to rage for more than five minutes. This stuff exhausts stage actors and they rarely smoke, let alone smoke Newport Menthol Kings and Dutch Masters cigars stuffed with low quality weed.

6. At this stage you may wish to offer your support as a way of helping him save face. You don't want to punk him out and then have him come back and shoot you. I have used some of the following:

Forging a Truce

I use "Sir," "man" or "young man" interchangeably to fit his age, so he doesn't feel like he's being played.

1. "Sir, are you okay? Do you need something to drink?" [Help him save face.]

2. "Sir, is there anything I can do for you?" [Do not use the term "help."] If he needs a job, offer to sit down and draw up his resume and give him a job lead. My competitor—Mister Mike, over in Hamilton—had many such men sent to him looking for work, and he never even thanked me!

3. "Sir, would you like to join for a reading of the Gospels? It's been a day since I opened myself to the Lord. I'd be glad"—by this time they're usually running. But just for authenticity's sake, I always have a copy of the New Testament in my backpack!

4. "Man, if you need to talk, I'm here for you."

5. "Sir, I would be willing to speak on your behalf to the police, so there is no misunderstanding about this."

6. "Don't be too hard on yourself, Sir. We all lose our temper sometime." That always got me a disbelieving look and usually the following, "Even you?" "Yes, even me. I just can't figure women out sometimes." Then they look up at you with a sparkle in their eyes, having found common ground and sympathy all at once, and you're richer by one more less than useless friend.

The main thing is to be steady, calm and unthreatening, behaviors that these people rarely see together and which encourages them to begin thinking before they speak, and thinking for such people is a herculean task—so help a brother out and be his Atlas. The ability to demonstrate respect [You can respect the space they occupy, at least.] and calm resolve in the face of verbal abuse, is the behavioral component of this method. The rest is simply a matter of body mechanics, of practicing the oblique position changes, something you can employee your irate mate for as she rants and raves about the myriad things that assail her peace of mind.

» Add a comment «

Sam J.   June 10, 2016 2:30 PM EDT

Thanks this is great advice. I see people getting wound up and clenching their fist like boxers. I see how this open handed stance is much better, less threatening, and still very effective. You can always close the hand before you hit him.

I've been thinking a lot lately about how all the fights I see on YouTube they now seem to start kicking the head when anyone goes down. I haven't been in a fight in a long, long time but I never remember anyone doing that. If someone went down and stayed that way it meant they were done and nothing else was needed. The point was made. Now they're trying to kill people. Stomping on someone's head probably has a high average of killing someone or at the very least brain damage.

Things are really getting out of hand and if Whites don't find some way of putting the fear of God in our enemies we'll go the way of the dodo.

At one time when Blacks or whoever attacked Whites hordes of Men would invade their space and start burning houses and kicking ass. Maybe not the most efficient way of going about things but it worked. We are eventually going to have to go back to some kind of serious retaliation tactic to bring back the fear.

Sam J.   June 10, 2016 4:25 AM EDT

"...3. Slowly raise your rear left hand so that your wrist touches your nipple and your hand is open toward him, over your shoulder, in front of your neck. You have just denied two kills targets in case he breaks out a knife and you're slower than him..."

I'm confused.

I think I got this but is it really...raise left hand palm facing towards the aggressor, over right shoulder in front of neck. Elbow at left nipple height.

or should the hand, facing the aggressor, be more towards the center of your body? Left?

I can't make my wrist touch my nipple and be over my shoulder at the same time. Maybe you've got really high nipples? :)

With the left hand up like this it protects the neck from knives and you can make a horizontal, upward or downward motion with the left hand to block his strong right hand strikes. Correct???

JL responds: June 10, 2016 12:47 PM EDT

What you want to accomplish with your left arm is to have the forearm in front of the heart off to the side, as the knife stab from a pocketed blade will come from an oblique inward arcing angle, and the slash will come at your neck—quite naturally, without intent—so you want your hand up there. With id all the way back and open it is not offensive, and if you have to fight, when you step off you already have the rear hand boxing—Jeet Kune Do guard up.

The tactical readiness you describe is on point.

You will ward off blows with your rear hand and keep him at bay with your lead hand. If he pulls a knife you sacrifice the left hand and bring the right hand in to get a double grip on his wrist or if he is bigger your step off and retreat behind your hands to the right.

If he is bigger and faster and has a knife, press the self-destruct button on your nuclear wrist watch and clatter your mandibles, with studied defiance, at him... These humans can be very lethal. That is, after all, why we come to this planet to hunt—for honor!

You don't want to lead with the left because your heart and aorta are on that side.

Sam J. June 9, 2016 11:29 AM EDT

This is really fantastic advice. Thank very much.

PR June 8, 2016 10:48 PM EDT

We need a video of this. Sell a DVD or .mp4 on Amazon.

Bottom Bitch

Doctor Landon, Please Resort to the Matriarchy Ward

So the topic of the day: What is a bitch? Hmmmmm? Not always a simple question to answer.

Well, for the Neanderthal man the bitch is the colloquial malicious, belligerent, coarse and spiteful creature. She is a bitch! Yeah, that sounds right. Of course, like most things this is a relative term since one man's bitch can be another man's bottom bitch. These being clearly uniquely distinct entities. The prostitute serving as the "bottom bitch" by the Neanderthal definition still holds a higher status than the standard everyday bitch of a woman who drives men crazy. At least the bottom bitch satisfies a need.

It does seem interestingly fitting that such a word came to our linguistic development. Literally meaning a female dog, the generic use now referring to an overbearing, distasteful woman somehow has the appropriate tone, even ring to it. Men everywhere have encountered the bitch in their day to day life. It is never a nice experience. This is so because there is no dealing with the BITCH, except of course for ignorance and indifference, which only potentiates the bitch mode of the BITCH even more thus contributing to the ultimate demise of the man to an emasculated wreck. I mean, you can't hit them: real men never hit a woman, even a bitchy one. They can't be vaporized in some sci-fi extravaganza, whereby they return as the porn goddess only interested in pleasing the Neanderthal through his every basic hedonistic need. NO, you see the bitch remains like the cockroach after the nuclear attack, or like fungus even after treatment.

So we are left with the only alternative, ignorance and indifference. But you see, herein lies the problem. Men can't let things be. WE are stupid that way. As well, indifference only feeds the bitch. It is an enigma. It can't be avoided; it can't be killed. It is JUST A BITCH.

So men do what men do. They attempt closure; fix and finish the problem. There has to be closure, an ending. The fire has to be put out. Once encountered the BITCH must be put in her proverbial place. Really, if it were another man being so, the Neanderthal would kick his ass and bam, bam thank you ma'am...closure, finite ending, the problem is resolved.

Elton John sang it and it was correct. "The Bitch is Back."

You see they never really leave because once a bitch always a bitch.

Clean the house?

Not good enough.

Mow the lawn?

Not good enough.

Multiple orgasms? Yeah, not good enough.

Do the dishes? Not good enough.

Polite respect... How dare you treat a woman like a woman—with respect!

Didn't you know men and women are equal, thus why women get away with being a bitch. Because they mistakenly assume we are equal (incorrectly so). Which is why we can't just kick your ass when you are a bitch and actually correct your problem as a BITCH!

So what do we do with the problem of the bitch? The Neanderthal man recommends the following basic points of advice:

1. Being a bitch is a disease. It is contagious. Be fearful but prepared to deal with it.

2. The disease can only be controlled but not cured.

3. Understand that the bitch, like the female dog, is preparing for sex, in heat for the mating process.

4. Treat your bitch with dignity, hard as it is.

5. The bitch is really guarding her soft fragile heart.

6. The bitch's heart is in need of coddling and attention.

7. So be nice, even in the face of danger and pain.

8. And finally, when in doubt.....JUST CUM ON HER FACE BECAUSE SOMETIMES THE BITCH JUST DESERVES IT!

Ha, Ha, Ain't that a BITCH

» Add a comment «

Kman June 13, 2016 2:29 PM EDT

Would love to hear the good Doctor's thought on the word/personage of Cunt.

'Human Rights for All'

A Harm City Poster Campaign

On every light pole on White Avenue, where I live in Caucasian splendor in the Hamilton area of Baltimore, which is 50% paleface, we have seen a number of posters, one of which sits on my desk. The one I did not take down had a picture of an African American woman of recent African extraction, in tribal dress, crying.

The poster on my desk is an 8.5 by 11 laminated affair and is dominated by a large red X with paintbrush effect and reads:

Gender Based Violence is Crime
Say NO to Gender Based Violence

Human Rights for All

I suppose this now means that those black women who are punching and kicking and slapping their small boys at the grocery store are now going to be served notice?

Is little Dante-done-been-whooped-a-million-times about to hear the bugle call of the cavalry coming to rescue him from his living hell?

How about little Jacobi, my neighbor, who is three and a half years old and was named after a Baltimore Ravens football player, who was traded to another team the very next season? Is some rescue team going to tell his mamma that she can't kick him out of the house from noon to sundown while she blows niggas in the basement?

On the bus, there was a poster that was a little more clear about what gender is in need of protection. Heading the ad is a sympathetic picture of a light-skinned black woman wearing a Maryland Judiciary visitors robe at a Maryland Court Self-Help Center and sipping coffee while she hides from her oppressor.

The poster reads:

-Child support

-Custody

-Divorce

-Landlord-Tenant

-Debt Collection

-Domestic Violence

-Small Claims

-Foreclosure

-Expungement

I'm confused. From the perspective of the five-year-old black boy who has been beaten and tortured by the cruel giantess who has bought an SUV with the money supposed to feed him, while he eats ramen noodles all month long, which one of the above points is for him?

Now, Little Brutha, I'm looking at number 9, Expungement, with some concern, as it seems to suggest that your mother may be a criminal—did you know your mamma beat the shit out of some poleese?

I know, son, that the child support thing sounds like a good deal for you. But all that is is the money that your mamma makes her car payment with and uses for liquor, cigarettes and shrimp and steak for herself and her boyfriends.

Of the nine things the Maryland Judiciary Self Help Center is intended to deal with, only the domestic violence issue would seem to favor Jacobi. Yet the picture of the person intended to be served looks a whole lot like his mother wished she looked like before she got knocked up with him at that Ravens football party!

And what five-year-old kid drinks coffee?

Where is the grape Koolade—dude, it's a trap! Ass whoopin' at one o'clock—duck and run, bro! Hurry, they got that bitch all fired up on caffeine!

'The Ritual Display of the Corpse'

SJWs Always Lie: Taking Down the Thought Police by Vox Day

2015, Castalia House, 234 pages

I don't usually read a book in an hour, but when I do, it's apparently one written by Vox day.

SJWs Always Lie is, perhaps, the most masculine book I have read, despite its origins among the whining, geek-infested halls of science-fiction nerds and videogame geeks.

Why?

Because this is a battleplan, a 100%, functional bundle of information exposing the enemy of the human mind—the simpering orthodoxy of those who would worship our faceless masters, for no other reason then they are deluded enough that when they look up to identify with their wretched fate, they see themselves reflected in divine hue.

Vox begins by introducing the conscience pimps of the media Left and their whores for what they are.

He then goes on to explain the three Social Justice Warrior laws, using concise examples.

The meat of the book is devoted to the operational principals of this wretched foe, and begins with a soul-searing quote by Theodore Dalrymple which ends with these two sentences, which for me, framed the entire political correctness debate in one soft voice;

"To ascent to obvious lies is to co-operate with evil, and in some small way to become evil oneself. One's standing to resist anything is thus eroded, and even destroyed."

This statement struck such a chord with me that I was embarrassed for having forgotten it, and worse, for not having these words remerge in my mind when confronted daily with the evidence that our entire society is built on interwoven lies of such vast complexity, that for the individual who is so insidiously cursed to dwell beneath them, the simple desire for the kind of peace of mind natural to the human leads him to this accursed juncture in the soul.

Vox then goes on to explain the operational doctrine of the enemy of all souls in the eight stage attack sequence favored by these orks of the mind. The attack sequence is focused on Violations of the Narrative, and is in-group aggression at its psychological apogee.

On page 137 we get the counter-offensive briefing a defender prefers if he's to stay focused and act effectively, especially when attacked by physically non-threatening foes. Though Vox does not couch this in terms of masculinity, his advice to never argue with the preening peacocks of The Lie is precisely that which any primitive man would have realized was the true course, but, which modern and postmodern man, has been kept from—the lion within himself—as a result of domestication and feminization. Don't bitch with bitches and you are halfway out of their clutches.

Ultimately I disagree on the quest for a safe place espoused in this book, for, if finally realized, such a quest will emasculate us again. That said, Vox Day has crafted a playbook that begs to be employed.

» Add a comment «

Kman   June 17, 2016 8:23 PM EDT

Vox takes the trouble to point out Aristotle's use of Rhetoric, as opposed to dialectic, for those " who cannot be instructed with information.

All part of a great book.

K-

Red Tex   June 17, 2016 2:28 PM EDT

Theodore Dalrymple is a master of "soul-searing" statements. I've read 2 of his books this year and was blown away by how he can boil down complex ideas and observations into one sentence.

The New Vichy Syndrome

Our Culture, What's Left of It

Not sure if you would agree with his personal philosophy, but the man can write extremely well.

Jeremy Bentham June 17, 2016 1:26 PM EDT

Good stuff James. I would say it is a must have self-defense manual for surviving the PC tyranny these days. We are, most of us, just one unguarded remark from losing our jobs, aren't we? If you are a Conservative, or even just neutral, the social justice warriors (SJW) of the Left want to get rid of you. To push you out of the organization, whether a business, school, church, government agency or even a gaming club. So if you slip up some day and use words like "crippled", "retarded" or "you people" the SJWs will want you fired forthwith, so they can replace you with a fellow SJW. Yes, it is indeed like "Invasion of the Body Snatchers" (i.e. Point and Shriek Attack). The main thing that Vox Day counsels is to stand strong. Don't resign, don't apologize, don't try to make nice with the SJW that are calling for your banishment to the metaphorical wilderness. Don't listen to people who will ask you not to "rock the boat". Once you find yourself targeted by the SJW it will be too late for that. If the SJW smell blood, sense weakness, nothing will placate them. The SJW are snakes, liars. Like the title says "SJW' Always Lie". They are at war, a holy war, a "Jihad", to remake society and YOU are the enemy, YOU are the Devil, YOU are in their way. Any lie they have to tell and any atrocity they have to commit will be justified in their own minds because they are working to create a Utopia. So conduct yourself accordingly when dealing with them. As Vox Day says the SJW are really cowards in the main who only have the courage of the mob. They really have trouble facing up to people who won't back down when they make their threat displays. Like Trump.

Eleven Crazy Bitches to Avoid

An Online Dating Service Has Selected the Right Women for the Taboo Harem!

Note that there are many spelling and abbreviation errors in the dating list. Those were copied and pasted directly from the site.

Seriously, six years ago, when I moved in here, I thought I would try dating online. Before I was done filling out my profile I was so disgusted with the process that I quit. Indeed, since I do not exist financially I could not even communicate with these babes if I wished. However, the freak show of sluts is quite entertaining. Finally, this week the bizzaro bitches went over the top. Basically, the pretty white girls are hookers, the black girls take pictures of their asses and the lonely white girls take pictures of their breasts for profiles.

NaughtySlut1

24F • Washington, DC

1 photo

[Breast picture-nice d-cup on small waist. Definitely a hooker.]

MsSnapperCrucial

26F • Upper Marlboro, MD

1 photo

Looking for occasional and clean fun. I am spoiled very ...

[This is the heaviest boned human I have seen outside of the Metrex World's Strongest Man Contest.]

Tyboogie555

28F • Baltimore, MD

1 photo

Ask me

[Not only is this average looking home girl content to be one of 555 identically daft bitches, she has taken her picture in the woman's room, striking a sexy pose in some public shitter.]

Cay_Cay

30F • Pasadena, MD

1 photo

Raised in Louisiana and recently moved to a new state. I like going ...

[This thin, redheaded, white girl looks like a stone-cold killer. I find her pretty—in a lethal kink way. I should be sterilized for even looking at this vampire bitch twice.]

Ladydiva54

54F • Havre de Grace, MD

1 photo

Single black ladies looking fro Mr. Right are you out ...

[To big black mammas who are entirely dressed in tasteful dresses and photographed in a plush residence and cannot spell—Oliver, if you would do the honors, I'm pretty certain they'd let us build a gym in the basement. It will get us closer to Philly and Jersey for your fights...]

rackadoom

30F • Lancaster, PA

1 photo

I'm here...about all I can say! I'm busy, don't freak out if I can't ...

[A life support system for a set of triple-Gs with a sense of humor. If I was still young I'd have Oliver fit me with a tracking beacon and repel into this bad idea from a Huey...with an oxygen tank!]

robyn337

110F • Washington, NC

1 photo

I'm Robyn looking for fun with another one or two or whatever hit me ...

[The clueless bitch that is content with being the 337th sista to have had her avian-inspired name misspelled by her ho mother wants to blow you, whoever, and how many of you, there happens to be. How utterly unappealing.]

bigmamawantsfun

54F • district hgts, MD

1 photo

Looking for a man/woman who not only says and knows he/she can eat ...

[This beast had the good taste not to post a pic at least.]

Pumpkin453

46F • Owings Mills, MD

[Another endlessly imaginative sister. Who lets these people name children?]

lolipopPrincess2

18F • Clinton, MD

1 photo

[This pretty little incubator would like you to upload a pre-neglected knockout game player so she can get a government apartment and get tattooed up—Oh, and she seems to have lost her candy stick.]

BigBootyT1110

37F · Owings Mills, MD

1 photo

Attractive BBW Interested in meeting someone for a little fun. A ...

[More prodigious, disembodied Caucasian breasts seeking companionship.]

» Add a comment «

Shep June 19, 2016 8:30 PM EDT

Photo of Cay_Cay? Strictly for training purposes, of course. So that we'll know what to steer clear of. Yeah, that's it...

JL responds: June 20, 2016 12:30 PM EDT

I can't post photos. Charles claims that this ability would herald the End Times.

She is thin, with a round face and pointed chin, straight light red hair, and would be pretty if not for those scintillant grey eyes that rip through you like a cat prowling by day.

Slick and the Ninja Bitch

A Cautionary Tale

Slick is an African immigrant who came over to Baltimore when he was a boy with his traditional, intact family. He began as the smart kid in school getting beat up for acting white and eventually devolved into a typical black Baltimore dude: working on and off, dressing like a thug and utterly lacking in discipline. His mother is horrified and has complained to Slick's friend that he is an embarrassment to the family and that African's do not act like this, to which his friend gave her a copy of the Vice video:

Cannibal Warlords of Liberia, which she is convinced is American propaganda!

In any case, one evening, Slick was, well, dressed up all, you know—Slick, sporting a brand new $200 pair of Air Jordan super sneakers. That girl he met at the club fell for him so hard it made his head spin. He took her home, banged her, and cruised off into sleepyville, another manly conquest under his belt...

In the morning [that's an hour after bedtime in Black America] Slick awakened alone, his window open.

His money was gone.

His Air Jordans were gone—out the window, in the hands of that thieving, ninja bitch, who had fallen in love with Slick's shoes and disciplined bitch that she was, did not let dick cloud her judgment, stayed on mission and made her way out into the profitable night posthaste, another notch in her lipstick case.

Lunch with Ian and Paul

A Brutha and a Redneck on 'Nasty Bitches' and other Pitfalls of the Bachelor Kind

Paul was a clerk from Wheeling, West Virginia, working in Baltimore with Ian and me, on a crew of about ten. These two older guys were telling stories about women back and forth, trying to shock each other. Ian was a black former Marine, who claimed to have been a member of a recon platoon. He made numerous claims that he and "the platoon" had done various things of the stupid kind. Two special ops soldiers have assured me that the majority of Marine Recon soldiers are above and beyond Ian's adventures. So, I suspect, that when Ian made a claim that he and "the whole platoon" went out to dip their wick in an unsavory skank well that he was referring to himself and the handful of other black recon soldiers in the unit in the late 1970s. In any case, Ian's adventures included:

1. Having unprotected sex with a Filipino whore after sneaking off base, and contracting VD.

2. Pulling a train on a hooker at her house near Paris Island, with him and his friends all contracting VD, getting needles shot in their ass, and then going back and getting VD from her again and getting needled again, because he, said, "the pussy was that good!"

3. Having sex with hookers in Okinawa at a place called "Shit River."

4. While stationed in Turkey at an American Airbase [Incrilik, I think] near the Syrian-Iranian border, Ian and his buddies had two days leave and wanted to get laid. Unfortunately, the nearest hooker was a day's drive inland. They rented a vehicle and drove out there, only to discover the hooker was ancient, 80 or more years old! Well, what is a soldier if he is afraid to soldier on in the face

of grim Fate? They had sex with her and felt they had gotten their money's worth.

5. Ian once picked up a cute looking girl on North Avenue, and decided to finger fuck her while he drove East toward Belair Road. When his hand slipped up her dress, he discovered that not only did she not have a vagina, but that her dick was bigger than his [which he indicated was more offensive than the fact that she had no vagina]. He let her off on the side of the road.

6. Once Ian got in an argument with his sister, which got physical. After he prevailed in the scuffle, he went to bed in his underwear, only to wake up to police batons raining down on his head as he was dragged out into the street while his sister talked trash to him about "...being a homeless nigger!"

With a "Beat that, white-boy" look on his face, Ian rested on his well-deserved laurels, confident that his life of bitches had been harder than Paul's. While Ian looked like Joe Frazier, Paul was a tall, lean, working machine, the best clerk I ever worked with. He was clean cut and wore button shirts and had a face like the actor that played the liquid terminator in T2: Judgment Day.

It turns out that Paul did once find himself necking at a night club in Atlantic City with a transvestite, and had to be restrained from throwing it out the window. He also spoke of a Gypsy woman in Wheeling, claiming that he and his teenage friends used to gather by the bushes on the side of her husband's house, and after her husband fell to sleep she would come out to the driveway and service them for a few dollars apiece.

The Bitch Next Door

In between jobs, Paul was staying back in Wheeling with his parents, who were both at work one hot, Ohio Valley, summer afternoon, when the young blonde from next door—who had been a little girl the last time he saw her—knocked on the screen door, a bottle of Jack Daniels in the crook of her arm. They sat and talked on the couch in the basement where he was staying: drinking, kissing, "grabbing ass" and eventually "getting to it."

This announcement brought Ian to attention as he clapped his hands together with a "Boo-yah muthafuca—boo-fucin'-yah" as he looked around at the other bruthas gathered about [none of whom I can recall by name, except for Monando Cay, the big West Indian.], as if to say, "This is how black dudes and real white boys come home, they take a woman!"

Paul then began describing how the girl went down on him and then climbed on his face and "rode" him, to which Monando smacked his lips in disgust and Ian quipped [this was back in the day when most black dudes would not eat pussy], "Sheeeeit, if she were white I'd eat that pussy too. A man don' eat pussy on Shit River, but a fine, young white bitch!"

Paul then got serious, explained how he had passed out drunk while she was rocking on his face and how he awoke in a panic, unable to see! He had been afraid that he was blind from the whiskey and panicked, crawling, feeling his way to the bathroom where he could turn on the light.

After flicking on the light, he was still unable to see and discovered that it was because his eyelids would not open.

[At this point, people stopped eating and Ian stopped cheering about what rambling men do to the bitch next door when they roll back into town.]

Paul then said [and I can recall these words], "My eyes were crusted shut, so I turned on the water and washed my face until I could see and it was a mess of blood, the sink filled with her period that had dried on my face."

A groan went up from the produce prep area where we were taking our lunch as a man threw his half eaten sandwich in the trash and Ian spit up a mouthful of food into the same can and said, after he wiped his mouth with the back of his hand, "Sheeeeit, I would a kilt dat bitch!"

Paul, a man with a temper, agreed and said it was his intention to slap her around when he knocked on her door. But that she apologized by way of a blow job and they called it even. The lunch area cleared with the shaking of heads, and I, a young man, barely 20, had been assured in gory detail by my lowlife, occupational elders, that a pedestal was no place for a woman.

Max Baer's Contract

Dealing with Two Bitches While You Have Two Slave girls in Bed

The following is part of boxing legendry from the days when the top ten earning American athletes would all be ring men, not ballplayers.

One time heavyweight champion, with a record of 70-13 with 52 KOs, Baer was a character out of the ring and literally a killer in the ring. He's the bad guy in Cinderella Man, a proud American Jew who was a smartass and wore a Star of David on his trunks, famously destroying German champ Max Schmeling at Yankee Stadium before 60,000 fans in 1933. He was one of numerous successful Jewish boxers of his time, including his brother, Buddy. Max's son played Jethro on the Beverly Hillbillies sitcom in the 1960s.

On one occasion he was in a hotel room bed with two women when two different promoters came to knock on his door—at cross purposes with one another—and began arguing in the hall while knocking for him, interrupting the ambiance of his tryst. He answered the door naked and invited them in to make their deal without delay. The two schemers then began to argue. Impatient to get back to his two lovelies, Max grabbed his frustrated member and beat it on the table, making an audible sound reminiscent of a judge's gavel, and demanded that order be observed in his court.

The two squabbling suits—who were, in fact, the two bitches in this story—were soon on their way, each with his portion of the made deal, and Max was able to return to the deal at hand.

On a less flattering postscript, Max was once being cornered by former Heavyweight King Jack Dempsey, against Joe Louis. Max was a tough dude. But as with many fighters that rely on a crushing punch, when they run into a bigger puncher, they lose heart. And so it was with Max as he crawled back to his corner after being floored again by Louis. Dempsey threatened to KO Max himself if he did not get up and go back out against the Brown Bomber, which he dutifully did, going down for the count in round 4.

Max would fight until 1941 and retired to become a boxing and wrestling referee.

Miss ReayQueen

Welcome to the BT-1000 Universe

Today I went to visit Dr. Philistine at his body garage along with the young lady who has harangued me to give the good doctor a visit for these past months. After the visit was over, well understanding that my motivation sat impatiently out in the lobby, Dr. Philistine preceded me and said in his most conciliatory tone, "He's going to die." He then briefed the lady and told her that I would be making a follow-up appointment to which she rose, shook his hand, and then as he used his hand to shield his eyes and pretended not to notice that the hourglass was overflowing, my hitherto obedient slave girl now demonstrated her insolent side and said, "So you haven't caused him any pain?"

He answered in the negative, and she declared that it was a shame, alluding to the fact that she might be dishing pain out soon enough, or at least this is how the top of the line Lexus model of the BT-1000 who was working behind the counter took my insolent slave girl's innuendo.

Miss ReayQueen could be a villainess in a Robert E. Howard story figure of the female with ebony skin and the long blond hair. She had shoulders like Tommy Hearns and a grin like Mohammed Ali, as she rose and exhorted my insolent slave girl to rise up and strike down her master, for this was the way of things, the way you handled your mens, "Unless of course you are his care giver," she said, with a smile to her and a meaningful shift in her eyes, to the two brothers sitting across from her in the corner in ever more cringing postures, "But if he's yours, you got to keep him in line, Sister."

Then, turning to me, she asked, "Do you want me to call you every 3-4 hours to see if you're still alive?" to which I took out my sunglasses and told her that I was already prepared for the abuse. At this point, I was just egging the lady on to the horror of the brothers and her white co-worker, and then, when we got outside, once again, comfortable in her subservient role, my slave girl said, "I think I got to meet a real BT-1000 who thought I was one of them too."

Let you this be a lesson to you bitches who aspire to be the slave girl of a true barbarian, that being on the arm of the non-conformed could bring you, too, the adoration and inclusion enjoyed by a true ebony queen.

Babes and Bitches

Management of the Post-Apocalyptic Barbarian Harem

Robert E. Howard and HP Lovecraft's old debate on the virtues of barbarism over civilization or vice-versa, is now a moot point, for savagery rules. So, this places the modern, aspiring barbarian warlord in the position of the socially evolving individual. As all the bitch boys and manginas proliferate around the emasculated world and continue to cast civilized bitches and savage bitches adrift, what's a barbarian pimp to do? On the one hand, you have your savage girls who think they are bitches yet aspire to be babes. On the other hand, you have your civilized girls who think they are babes but are in fact raging bitches. [We are leaving out the vast majority of females, savage bitches who will never be babes and civilized women who aspire only to dominant bitchdom. Since we only have two hands, that leaves these girls out, and if you did have a third hand, rest assured that it would be palming the top of a head.]

Seriously, back to the trainable girls who matter, what you want to achieve is a babe who thinks she is a bitch. Follow these easy steps given to me by my fighter, Oliver, who carries business cards in his wallet, not one of which has ever been given out on a business call, because he takes care of that on a smart phone. The business card is the invitation for the wannabe babe.

After she is firmly addicted to your kindness, your firmness, your harsh, firm address of her soft mystery, after many a door has been held dotingly for her, after rude men have been cast off her scent with a meaningful glare, begin her slave girl training.

a. With your arm firmly around her, say, "I love you, Bitch."

b. With your hand soothingly on the back of her neck, feeling her most powerful as she knows that your manhood is firmly within the jaws of judgment, say "You're a beautiful Bitch."

c. Some hours later, while she's unable to breathe, and you can tell that she's really hot, truthfully say, "You're such a hot Bitch."

d. While you're at your brother's wedding and your arms around her, be sure to whisper in her ear with inverted sincerity, "Bitch, I love you."

e. After you have treated the fine lady to her first two-digit orgasmic experience (for you Nimrods who think we're referring to fingers here, this is 10 or more orgasms in one unmasking of her interior), pretend to rise out of bed to head for the beer cooler, but do so with a pained look like you've fought too many fights, smacked down too many chumps, walked away from too many ho's, your training will come to fruitiion as she says, "No, Baby, I'll get that." Then, when she brings your beer back, crack it open, then thoughtfully kiss her before you take a drink, offering her a draught first and then say, with all adoring sincerity, "You're such a good bitch."

f. At this point, if you've gotten this far, the other sixteen steps will be a breeze and will progress according to your sexual prowess. Just know that in the end, at the end of that curvy rainbow, the goal is that when you're thirsty and you've had a rough day at work, all you have to do is cast an admiring eye on your slave girl and say, "Bitch, a beer."

How to Marry

The Bitch Who is Already Beating You

Mike, who is bipolar and used to do crack, but has straightened his life out enough to have a steady girlfriend for the past five years, just got married. I talked to Ellen, who was at the wedding yesterday, and told me that her new stepfather did not show up with the usual black eye or two, so things have apparently been blissful in Wicked Bitchland. However, Ellen did relate Mike's condition in such a way as to indicate that our heroic groom might have been fearing the return of hard domestic times.

Mike, who normal operates a dump trunk, but had off of work for his wedding this Friday, arrived at the Towson Courthouse at 9 a.m., with his father, both of them appropriately drunk for the occasion. In fact, when the County official presiding over the ceremony asked if any one present had any objections to the union, Mike's dad raises his hand and said he did—and then retracted the motion with a "Just kidding, Sue!"

Well, there you go young men, learn from Mike, if the bitch is already punching you in the face on a regular before you tie the knot, you might just as well show up at your sentencing drunk. Really, dude, if you must, do it drunk!

Rosalie

An Authentic Baltimore Icon on Back Alley Zumba, Dindu Academia and the Blooming Race War

Rosalie is a Northeast Baltimore original, a retired math teacher and the former hostess of an authentic Italian restaurant, which closed not long ago because of Dindus robbing patrons out front. She was once a customer of mine when I was a supermarket manager. I ran into her today in front of the Fenwick Bakery in Parkville on the City side of the line. With some Baltimoreans you only need to ask them how they are doing and you get an earful, in public, as the Dindus walk by, giving her "you can't say that" looks.

Enjoying the race war, darling. You know we live in a communist country. People think I'm crazy when I say that. But we are being made to do everything we don't want to do and have everything done to us by the people that are above the law. I was going to get back into teaching but they don't want white teachers anymore, not even out in the county. Everything is going black. My grandchild is only one of eleven white children in the entire school and he gets attacked by these little shits every day. My baby goes to school to learn, because it's the law, and these turds with arms and legs swarm him like flies swarm on them. Of course the teacher looks the other way. What's she going to do, go against her own?

You know the Bel Loc Diner is closing. It's going to be a Starbucks. Not in time though. Last year my niece was beaten to death in the alley by niggers, right behind the diner. I'll die by a nigger hand too, because I'm not backing down from these fucking animals.

Last night, in the alley behind my daughter's house—I live with my daughter now to help with the children—we have these so-called upscale middleclass blacks, four pretty coons with their hooped earrings and fake braids all the way down to their asses, reciting a Zumba performance in the alley. I shit you not, baby. These bitches had a fucking PA system hooked up in the alley! I was gardening because it was still light out, had my shovel. But the baby was sleeping. There is no speaking to these people. So my daughter calls the police and a cop comes. He is standing their telling her he can't do a thing even though it's against the noise ordinance. If they don't want to move he can't move them. He's not supposed to lock anybody up, just speak to them, mediation.

Now, the entire time the cop is talking to my daughter, these whores are threatening her for calling the cops, so I flip them the finger. Then they start complaining to the cop that I flipped them the finger. He asked me if I did, so I asked the leader bitch what finger I flipped her, and she said, "The middle finger."

I said, "Congratulations, that's the third finger. I didn't think you could count that high."

So she says, "Oh, you a smart bitch, huh? Well, you a fat bitch too. You oughta be taken our Zumba."

Oh, I knew I had her then, thought maybe she'd come across the alley at me. I said, "No, Baby Girl, I get enough exercise riding your husband's big black cock for eight hours a day while you're at work. It's awful nice of you to let him stay home to take care of Old Rosalie!"

[Hysterical laughter as a bystander looks on with fear as Rosalie gestures expressively, her eyes widening, her volume climbing.]

Let me tell ya, baby, that tweety-bird bitch was ready to bring it, started across the alley swinging her braids so you could hear them slap on that hard monkey ass of hers. Well, the cop is holding her back and the other bitch is eye-balling me, so I tell her, "Come on, I'll bury your ass with this shovel, bitch!"

She starts telling the cop, "She threaten me, officer, she threaten me!"

Of course, the cop is stupid, but he's not a complete idiot, and did overhear me say something, so he turns to me and says, "What did I hear you say, Miss?"

I turned on the Rosalie charm, batted my eye lashes at him and said, "Oh, excuse me for interrupting, Officer Handsome, but I was just saying to my neighbor that "Burying this grass with this shovel is a bitch."

Baby, I don't say shit around a cop unless I have an alternate version. Those whores were fit to be tied. My daughter and girlfriend keep getting on me about back-talking the niggers, but I like black people, so it's pretty damned hard for me to put up with niggers. I'm standing my ground. On my tombstone it 'ill read, "Here lies Rosalie, killed for back-talking niggers."

I understand that people will have a variety of opinions on Rosalie, and she would understand as well—and tell you exactly where your opinion belongs. But what struck me the most about this story—told on a sidewalk while pedestrians gave us a wide berth—was how much it must suck to be a Baltimore City Police officer! Look, I hate pigs as much as the next irascible misanthrope, but I have to pity any cop that has to referee such altercations. After a few years of this kind of action I think I'd be primed to shoot first and ask questions later.

Note: there is no truth to the rumor that Rosalie was the inspiration for the AC-DC song "Whole Lot a Rosie." The song was inspired by a Baltimore woman, who I also knew, but briefly, who was a stripper, not a teacher-hostess.

» Add a comment «

Sam J. July 14, 2016 12:39 AM EDT

"...Last year my niece was beaten to death in the alley by niggers, right behind the diner..."

I feel for this lady. It made me very sad to hear this.

Shep July 12, 2016 9:24 PM EDT

How much it sucks to be a policeman in ANY city in modern America. This happens on every shift in every city of any size on the Left Coast, and the rules of engagement are the same. I don't know why any Caucasian would want to do that job any more.

'The Rabbit People'

100 White Women a Day Versus 10 Black Women a Year: Jeremy Bentham on Interracial Rape

The most traumatic aspect of my first sexual experience was the fact that the woman under me, who had seemed so in control of every aspect of our interaction until docking was achieved, began squealing like a dying rabbit, a sound I had just heard days before as I pulled an arrow from the body of a still flopping bunny. I don't know if Jeremy read that piece or not, but he really infused me with a creepy state of clarity in this following piece. Oh, in defense of the oppressed, 95% of black women who enroll in U. S. colleges, have already been raped, the survey says...

Hey James,

Speaking of Anonymous Conservative...As you have pointed out from your personal experiences James, many women, even many rabid Feminists, have the hot's for violent men. Most of the rest of us reading your blog have observed the very same phenomenon. What these women really want sexually is clearly different from what they say they want. WHY IS THAT? This insane dichotomy has always been a head scratcher, hasn't it? Well Anonymous Conservative offers a cogent explanation for this contradictory behavior: it is evolutionary reproductive strategy. It is hard-wired into the brains of "r/strategist" women such that it isn't a conscious decision on their part. It is "genetic drive". How the distant ancestors of these r/strategist women spread their own genes throughout the human gene pool: by producing offspring by rapists or seducers who went on to spread the women's own traits by further rape and/or seduction. As it is, in many third world cultures rape is merely regarded as "physical seduction" after all. Those Western women wouldn't be lying naked on the beach if they didn't really "want it", now would they?

New Rape Defense: I Wasn't Listening, So I Never Heard Her Cries

Posted on July 16, 2016 by Anonymous Conservative

Women will need to learn that as a practical matter, with regard to rape, they can bring it on themselves now and the man will be blameless:

A woman sunbaking naked was sexually assaulted by a Kenyan migrant who attacked her as she lay on a nudist beach with a hat covering her face...

Magistrate Leanne Atkins considered a prison sentence for Kimutai but decided on 180 hours of community service work and to be subjected to an 18-month 'Intense Supervision Order.'

...His victim, who was not identified, was sunbaking naked at the beach when Kimutai, who was also naked, approached her...

The woman moved away but Kimutai followed her into the ocean.

While swimming near her she told him to 'go away and leave me alone'.

The woman moved back to the beach where she was sunbaking naked with a hat over her face when Kimutai indecently assaulted her...

She screamed and told her attacker to leave her alone.

Why was the sentence so light? The rape wasn't his fault. Why you ask?

Kimutai did not listen to the woman, Magistrate Atkins said.

So he only got 180 hours of community service. Since he isn't employed, that is 18 days of ten hours a day, and then he is right back on track for citizenship.

Feminists need to know that no doesn't mean no anymore, if the man is not listening.

This is great for me. I never listen to women anymore. When I am around them the only sound I hear is the noise Charlie Brown hears when his teachers talk to him. All I hear is, "Waahhh Weeehhh Wooohhhh wooohhh waahhh WiiiiiHHHH wiiiihhhh Wahhhh." I had no idea that I now have a license to act like Bill Clinton and just rape whoever I want.

Truth be told, from a game perspective, it makes perfect sense. Who listens to women? Betas and Gammas. Alphas assume that most of the shit women say is just pulling their chains. To an Alpha, a woman's opinion is just an opportunity to playfully poke fun at her and make silly analogies in the attraction phase, and to nod yes to, in a sincere fashion while maintaining intense eye contact, in the comfort phase. Thus this legal defense is basically a way to confer rape-immunity on Alphas, while making sure every gamma and beta is still forced to beg for sex, endure the inevitable denial, and then get sent out for coffee and bagels.

Think about it. Feminists want men to be imprisoned for wolf-whistling in Britain, but they are totally silent about this case. This is legal codification of rape-immunity for alphas, acceded to by feminists through the silence of the feminist movement. No doesn't mean no, if you are not listening.

This is because r-selected rabbit women secretly want to be raped by alphas who ignore their pleas for mercy. When that happens, their genes will be mixed with a bold rapist's, and their rapist children will be more likely to forcefully impregnate numerous innocent women themselves, carrying their genes forward. That is called genetic drive.

This leftist judge probably views being sexed up against her will by some foreign cretin who ignores her cries as a tingle-filled fantasy, so in her opinion this case was not a real crime, the same way Roman Polanski's rape of a twelve year old wasn't really "rape-rape", according to Whoopi Goldberg.

In truth, if this nude sunbather didn't want to be raped, why did she stay, naked on the beach, when this naked migrant was chasing her around and ignoring her pleas to be left alone? What woman, naked and vulnerable, remains around a naked foreign man who is ignoring everything she says? What woman, naked and vulnerable in that situation, lays out naked, with a hat over her head so she can't see what is going on around her? According to the Australian legal system, by her actions, she made this rape excusable.

Human r-strategist women have a deep evolutionary brain program that is designed to get them raped. Whether it is female artists going to Cologne after the rapes and walking around naked, or naked sunbathers who remain naked around aggressive men who won't take no for an answer, they subconsciously are seeking the same thing - rapist babies.

Leftist insanity can only be understood through the prism of reproductive strategy. Logic, reason, and common sense have no role in understanding them.

http://www.anonymousconservative.com/blog/new-rape-defense-i-wasnt-listening-so-i-never-heard-her-cries-for-help/

http://www.dailymail.co.uk/news/article-3691160/Woman-sunbathing-naked-nudist-beach-sexually-assaulted-Kenyan-migrant-24-near-Warnbro-Western-Australia.html

Naturally posting this inconvenient truth will likely earn you a lot of backlash from the bunny rabbit people, James. Hear the shriek of the wounded rabbit! It attracts predators like nothing else will.

https://www.youtube.com/watch?v=fDBgP83Sizo Stoat kills rabbit.

https://www.youtube.com/watch?v=HNbqvqf3-14 BBC- Stoat kills rabbit ten times its size.

Regardless of any precedent this particular case might set, keep in mind that white men are held to a higher standard of behavior by Leftists and Cuckservative white knights alike. White men are expected to be much more capable of "self-control" by the Leftist dominated criminal justice system, both at home and abroad, and thus can be expected to be punished accordingly for any sexual transgressions, real or imagined. The Leftist bigotry of lower expectations on display: http://www.israelnationalnews.com/News/News.aspx/214479#.V31q17grJhE (Swedish Politian: Migrant rape isn't as bad).

Note as well that the way the FBI's Uniform Crime Report (UCR) breaks down the number of forcible rapes committed in the USA annually, a total 10 black women will be raped by white men in the USA each year, whereas

100 white women will be raped by black men each and every day. Yet the current Leftist narrative is that there is a threat of rape on college campi being perpetrated exclusively by "white frat boys". Oh yeah?

So what you see going on around you daily guys is the war of the "bunny rabbit" people" against the "wolf" people (AKA Leftist "Goodwhites" versus Conservative "Badwhites") . Resources are currently abundant so "rabbit" values suited for exploiting times of glut are often more attractive to the public at large than "wolf" values designed for survival in times of shortage (i.e. Leftist values versus Conservative values). The rabbit people are selfish cowards who are incompetent to lead or even survive themselves in times of scarcity. The rabbit people are self-aware enough to understand that they cannot compete against wolf people on anything resembling even terms. Thus the rabbits are using every dirty trick they can muster to disadvantage the wolves while they can. This includes employing proxies to do their fighting for them. Proxies like big government and violent outsiders that can outnumber and overpower the wolves. Much like real rabbits, the bunny rabbit people have NO loyalty to their own in-group, their herd, their warren, their "fluffle", tribe, race, religion, ethnicity or country. As long as the "stoat" lets them live, eat grass and fuck that's all they care about. They'll just stand by and watch the stoat kill other rabbits. No matter how much the other rabbit shrieks they won't make a move to help. They'll even help the stoat get other rabbits if they should imagine it will keep them on the stoat's good side.

If you're a "wolf" man who has been looking for a life mate and can't seem to find a suitable one among all the "bunny rabbit" women, now you know why. But take heart, you are NOT the only "wolf" out there. Hear the pack howl!

"For the strength of the Pack is the Wolf, and the strength of the Wolf is the Pack."

- Rudyard Kipling, "The Law of the Jungle - The Jungle Book" (1894).

https://allpoetry.com/The-Law-Of-The-Jungle

Blatant Bitches

Shane, Queenita and the Dirtbag

Shane is an older middle aged paleface, a Vietnam Vet, who keeps in shape, has a decent job, and has a sweet girl—eh, and a wife. Well, he and the wife don't get physical anymore, each figuring the other is probably having their intimacy taken care of somewhere else. His girl is young and no way does he need another kid, so he always puts on a "rain coat."

Unfortunately—though fortunately for the pride of the Caucasian race in Shane's small corner of the world in Parkville, Maryland—he was blessed with two things, a strong heart...and a cinema-worthy endowment. [Shane blushes as he obliquely refers to this in conversation, regarding it as something of a curse.] The problem is, finding the right size at the 7-11 on the way to his girl's early in the morning before work, is not always easy. Most places do not even carry his size, so he swings into the city and hits the 7-11 there, where the brothers shop.

Once, late at night, he used the Giant over in Ravenwood. Shane stood patiently behind a young black couple as they argued over whether or not to buy the condoms with the "ribs on them." He became impatient, what with his girl waiting in the car and his wife waiting up to watch the Jimmy Falon show with him, so said, "Excuse me," and reached between the squabbling youngsters and took the last box of Magnum Extra Large off the shelf, to which the young girl's eyes popped open wide as she checked out Shane, and then darted narrowly to her ever-shrinking man and sneered, "Ribbed, you weak-ass nigga." She then flashed a plastic smile at Shane as her man complied in abject humiliation to her request for artificially enhanced girth, and said as sweet as could be, "Have a nice night, sir," then ripped into her man again, "En he payin' for dat shit too, boy, while I payin' ta bag yo weakass shit!"

Shane, who had harbored black girl fantasies, never felt that way again after hearing that, just imagining how much the pillow talk would remind him of getting stuck up by that Puerto Rican on the parking lot of the CVS drugstore.

Queenita and the Dirt-bag

Usually the African guy at the counter just sneers at him when he makes his $4.99 purchase for a 3-pack. But this past Thursday morning, before the sun rose, he faced embarrassment on a different scale. A tall, pretty black girl with the face of that Ethiopian model that was popular in the 1990s, and a fit, figure greeted him with a smile, obviously indicating this was her first week on the job.

Shane stepped aside to let the junkie looking white dude with all the tattoos, left over from the previous night, ahead of him. But the guy motioned that he was not ready yet. Immediately suspecting that this dirt-bag might be fixing to rob the joint, he kept one eye on him the entire time, [1] and, kind of embarrassed over being a basically ancient dude buying condoms at the 7-11 in front of these two twenty-somethings, pointed at the condom rack.

The young lady spoke clearly, "A box of condoms, sir?"

He looked at the dirt-bag, who stopped rooting in his pockets for change at those words, and after they both made eye-contact, looked back at the young lady and nodded meekly.

She replied with a very professional demeanor, "What selection, sir."

He mumbled, "The black box."

She looked at him directly and said, "Magnums, sir, what kind?"

The dirt-bag was straight up staring at him as he held out his hand and held up two fingers.

A smirk crossed her face as she said, at a normal conversational tone that rang like a loud speaker at 5 a.m. in this empty 7-11, "Extra-Large, sir."

He nodded affirmatively as he took out his wallet, keeping an eye on the dirt-bag, and handed her a $5.

The woman halted, before ringing up the purchase, tapped on the counter where was pasted the face of the 7-11 actor portraying the 30-year-old dude that must be carded to buy cigarettes, and said, "I'll need to see your I.D., sir."

The dirt-bag jerked his head as if he had been struck, as Shane's mouth gaped at the woman, and she said, in a very professional tone, "Please, sir, it's the law."

The dirt-bag, who had been developing eye-contact report with Shane, mouthed "what-the-fuck," as Shane handed over his I.D., to which the young lady suddenly became most unprofessional, leaning forward until she was prone on the counter on her elbows, one propping up her chin with the $5 between the fingers and the other holding the Maryland State I.D., which she waved, "Mister Man Shane, lives right around the corner. Isn't that convenient for lonely Queenita."

The dirt-bag let out a grunt as Shane stood dumbfounded, realizing that this ghetto bitch now knew where he lived and could walk right up to his front door and.—"I'm married," he blurted.

Her seductive smile then melted and she returned the I.D. and rang up the purchase as she said, "That's a Shame, Mister Man Shane, because I'm not a ho, and we'll have to pass on what might have been."

Her smile made him think that she was some kind of comedian, that she was enjoying this way too much, like his wife put her up to it or something. Then, after ringing up the sale and placing the penny in the hand with the box, she held it pack with a wry grin and said, "I have to know."

The dirt-bag was just standing, gawking, and Shane gave him an indignant look, to which the dirt-bag shrugged his shoulders as if Shane's intimate business were public property.

Dumfounded, he said to the smirking girl, younger than his daughter by a decade, "I don't understand."

She then smiled openly and placed the heels of her hands on the counter and said, "Come on, I know you all men name your critter. I just want the name and you can have your pro-tect-ion."

Dumfounded, he stood back and looked at both of them, suddenly having the impression that he was in an asylum. The dirt-bag broke the ice, "I'll go first. I ain't proud."

Queenita snorted, "Okay, let's hear it—no strings attached, alright."

The skinny little man with the Mickey Mouse tattoo on the back of his hand and a black heart on his throat, put his hands up next to his neck and did some hand flourish and said, "Vanilla Nice!"

Queenita, who was winning Shane over as a person with her bizarre but in control sense of humor, said, "Not bad—I believe that's original, and most importantly, is not too boastful. You have no idea how many times I've had to hear, 'Here comes Big Johnson,' as if he was the first dude that named his critter that."

They then both stared, looking up at him expectantly, like his children had on Christmas morning. He shrugged his shoulders in embarrassment, and the dirt-bag assured him, "It's all good, Pops. We're all friends here."

Queenita winked at him, which gave him the courage to name his totemic mating image and he answered her as he extended his hand for the box, "Jaws."

Queenita handed him the box with her mouth open, her eyes wide and uncomprehending, as the dirt-bag laughed in a gargling fashion and gave Shane a high-five, "Fucking right, Pops!"

The dirt-bag then noticed that Queenita did not have a clue, and as Shane stepped to the door he said, "It was a movie about a great white shark that ate bitches and boats, yo!"

To this Queenita stepped back and pumped her fist in the air, laughing in a high-pitched squeal and stomping one foot, smiling like she had just added a valuable to some rare collection. [2]

There is no real moral to this story, but was too damned funny not to preserve in a book about bitches, of which the 'blatant" variety had not originally figured into the outline.

Notes

1. Shane thought for sure that this guy was going to rob him or the store.

2. Shane mentioned, by way of comparison, the look on his friend's face in 1968 when he added Baltimore Orioles, first baseman, Boog Powell's card to his baseball card collection.

» Add a comment «

dcjuggler   July 22, 2016 1:45 PM EDT

The Shane/Queenita story is Hall-of-Fame worthy.

Serious Bitches

Chauvinistic Therapy Resistance

Today I was finishing with my doctor's visit when he asked me, "Is she out there?" After I responded in the affirmative, he said, "I'll take care of that for you." He then proceeded boldly out into the hen den, that is, the administrative and waiting area and addressed She. "He's alive." To which She responded, "Still?"

My doctor advocate then addressed She with her nursing instructions: "Take good care of him, cook him steak, get him his beer, keep the house clean, and make sure he is otherwise provided for. This is the chauvinistic therapy regimen."

She said, "Don't worry, I will—he takes advantage anyway, you know."

And up rose the leader of the estrogen resistance, a top of the line BT-900, wearing a shawl and as lithe as a villainess in a Robert E. Howard yarn. Turning her attention to She, this woman pulled open a drawer at the base of her desk and said, "I've got the pistol right here, honey, to cure what ails him."

We had a laugh, although the estrogen leadership was not smiling in the wake of her sardonic laughter, and as I waved goodbye to her leaving the door, she said to me, "Give me a call and let me know how that works out for you," assured that her marching orders would be implemented by her acolyte.

The postmodern barbarian warlord must understand that his sweet little slave girl or worshipful priestess is but the flower that buds on the end of a branch of a vast, intertwined, ever-growing, feminist organism. Where the roots of this thorny, vining estrogen shrub sink into the earth is the trunk, the ineradicable root of the estrogen resistance, personified by that woman with the pistol in her desk drawer. Be careful, in dealing with management of your babe, to consider that this woman, the shrill voice, may act upon your babe in times of stress and transmogrify your lovely little property into thorny swampland.

Slick Bitches

Miria Benitez' Sixth Sense

I had a breakfast with the lovely Miria Benitez, an educator with a PhD, a really smart bitch. I made a dinner date with her for 4pm. Just as she dropped me off at the front door of the gladiator barracks, knowing that I was working on my writing, she offered to stay and help, but I declined, chivalrously resisting that I soujourn alone on my literary problems, not wishing to impose upon her large brain, failing to consider that this negligent act on my part left all that considerable cerebral wattage free to dwell on an unlikely conspiracy theory that I may have in fact declined her offer of aid in order to entertain a lady friend. I had not calculated that the large brained female has a peculiar ego of its own. Although Miria Benitez knew that I entertained Mrs. Bedwrecker once a week, it irritated her to no end, that I would not let her know when. I saw this as simple prudence, not wanting a cat fight on the front lawn, which could result in both of the lovelies being marked up, kind of like sideswiping your Camaro with a Trans Am that you only drive on Sundays. Señorita Benitez, on the other hand, saw this as an insult to her intelligence, that I would be so audacious as to insinuate that she would not be able to figure out the day and the hour on her own.

I, on the other hand, was fully confident that I would have plenty of time to get my work done and have time between dates to freshen up. After all, what could go wrong?

At 4:55, I woke up to the sound of my bedroom door opening and of my head pounding, from the bottle of bedwrecking wine that I had not planned on arriving at my door in a leather purse. Immediately cognizant of my compromised situation, I glanced around and noticed that there were no condoms stuck to the end table or on the floor, and surmised that I had properly disposed of them in the waste basket and patted myself on the back mentally—free and clear.

As the lovely Latina crawled into bed with me, I heard her sniffing, and the doors of hell opened wide. As she said, "You've been drinking—in the middle of a writing day?!"

I rolled over and moaned, not knowing what line of bullshit I could pull out of the back of my head while it was pounding, to explain my obvious and uncustomary lack of writing discipline, nevertheless, still able to silently breath an almost-got-busted whew of relief that she had smelled wine and nothing more incriminating.

Then, the lovely nose sniffed again—off of one hook and onto another, and she said, "I smell latex." I rolled over and groaned, as she crawled down lower in the bed. As I covered my eyes with my hairy forearm, I heard furious sniffing coming from the nether regions of the bed, as if I were a chain gang runaway listening to the slave master's hound dogs sniff out my trail without a handful of pepper in sight...

There was a deep breath followed by a deep knowing sigh of affirmation. Then, like an archeologist confirming his suspicions on a Neolithic dig, the lovely Latina declared, "I smell pussy."

She then crawled back up and under the guise of coming in for a kiss, she sniffed my beard and said, "And, you've been eating it."

At this point, feeling like Goldilocks with her face in the porridge, I used the hand of the arm that she was laying upon to arrange the pillows in the upper corner of the bed so as to offer maximum concealment for the bowie knife I keep under there for that day when my many enemies come bursting through the door, not wanting to go out like Agamemnon. She was a Latina, after all.

To my surprise, she seemed giddy with victory, happy to be with me, cuddly, but not in a bunny rabbitish sort of way, more in the manner of a great fuzzy snake that loves you for now. She just needed to know, smug in her confidence—to an extent that I felt like a mouse that the cat had so enjoyed catching, he was being released for another go without even getting raked by her claws.

I write this as a lesson to you married men who may have made the mistake of trying to up the IQ of your offspring by marrying a brilliant bitch. Make sure that you have sown your wild oats, because we wouldn't want anything to happen to the sowing device.

Drunk Bitches

Chili Boy Joe and Aunt Margie

Joe was recently at a party of the Caucasian kind. Upscale Caucasian, not that low-rent shit. Joe, though, is Jamaican. He attended the party with a platonic lady friend. Also at this party was the former boyfriend of his date, who is newly married. Part of the reason why Joe was there, was to keep the newly married, former boyfriend away from the young lady, who had grown tired of his continued attentions after marriage. The ex-boyfriend and the date both became very drunk. Joe became involved in conversations with the other party goers as his date wandered from room to room, trying to get away from her ex-boyfriend, whose wife was also at the party.

The wife, was so upset over the attention that her new husband was paying to his ex-girlfriend, that she got so drunk that she passed out in the room where all the coats were laid out. In the meantime, Joe's date was nodding out on the couch having drunk so much that she was barely conscious. Joe kept an eye on the situation and was shocked when the ex-boyfriend, finding his wife passed out drunk in the other room, came to his date and began coaxing her to get up and go out to his car with him. Not wanting to be the black guy beating up the white guy at the white party in the all-white neighborhood, Joe picked his date up and carried her out to his own car and drove her home.

His date passed out drunk on the way home. Joe had a hard time waking her up once he arrived at the house where she lived with her family. He retrieved her keys from her purse, heaved her over his shoulder and carried her up both flights of stairs to the back door. He did not want to be seen hauling a limp, white woman around this neighborhood. As Joe carried up to the back door and began to unlock it, he had nightmare thoughts about what he would do to any negro he saw hauling his daughter up the stairs and hoped her father didn't have a gun.

To Joe's relief, the back door was opened for him by the girl's mother, who invited him in, walked him upstairs to her bedroom, held the door open while he laid his friend down on the bed, and then said, "I think you kids need some alone time," and shut the door.

Joe told me, "Here I was, afraid the family was going to shoot me for hauling their daughter around, and they're giving her away. She was really out of it and wanted to have sex with me, but I'm not going to have sex with a drunk girl, especially somebody I didn't get together with for that purpose. She asked me to lay with her and hold her, so I did, until she fell asleep. Then I went downstairs. When I went downstairs, there was another woman there, who was drunk. It was the aunt. It was a houseful of pussy. Mom, the aunt, and the daughter, all single. Mom asked me to stay, because she was cooking chili, so I stayed and ate the chili, while the aunt drank and looked at me. Eventually, I'm drinking too, on the couch, with the aunt, while mom's taking pictures of us, like I'm a teddy bear, and posting it on her Facebook, titled, 'chili boy.' They kept calling me their chili boy. I eventually fell asleep on the couch and woke up the next morning while the aunt was fixing me breakfast, eggs and cheese. So that was my Saturday night."

In our emasculated day and age, there are ever more all-female households. On every block in your neighborhood, there's gonna be a hen house. Whether you're going to take advantage of this is entirely up to you. Chili boy had better things to do.

» Add a comment «
Jeremy Bentham July 25, 2016 6:50 PM EDT

B is right. Cigareets n' whisky n' wild, wild women... they'll drive you crazy...they'll drive you insane...

https://www.bing.com/videos/search?q=cigarettes+and+whiskey+and+wild+wild+women&&view=detail&mid=A86C27F21E21B4B38CBFA86C27F

21E21B4B38CBF&FORM=VRDGAR

But wasn't that a party?

https://www.bing.com/videos/search?q=wasn%27t+that+a+party+song&qpvt=wasn%27t+that+a+party+song&FORM=VDRE

B July 23, 2016 6:25 PM EDT

Chauffeuring around drunk bitches whose life is a mess is a good way to go to jail or otherwise get involved in their mess (for instance, by getting clocked in the back of the head by an upset ex.)

Any female that tells you about what an asshole her ex was, or otherwise tries to involve you in the dog's breakfast that is her personal life is an instant write-off. In this case, it's obvious that this bitch was hoping to get your friend involved in a fight with her ex, in order to vicariously enjoy the sight of two primate males fighting over her. That's the kind of shit that a woman raised by a single mother thinks is a good idea. He's an idiot and patsy for going, and is lucky he didn't end up in a world of shit. The proper response is "a great way to avoid your ex at this party is to spend the evening cooking me dinner at my house." Give her a manageable task with a clear reward on a short timeline.

Bars and parties are a bad, bad place. A hostile environment full of drunk strangers, some of whom are assholes, where you are expected to drink. I mean parties in the American sense, not like a group of friends getting together.

I don't think I've ever materially improved my life, met someone who turned into a good friend, or learned something new at one of these.

And I'm lucky—I never had anything bad happen as a result of this shit. No DUIs, no knocked out teeth, no nothing. But I have had plenty of friends who did. One guy got in a fight in a bar and got his ear bit off-now he's got to walk around for the rest of his life with a missing ear. Another (an SF guy) had a friend mouth off to a bouncer, got involved, got jumped by bouncers in the parking lot, and was being choked out from behind by one of them when he decided to fix the problem by stabbing the guy in the leg. Well, in the short term, he fixed the problem. In the long term, he ended up being tried and had to plea to a misdemeanor assault to avoid a felony conviction. Etc, etc.

I can barely remember the last time I've been in a bar or at a stranger party, and don't miss it in the slightest.

responds: July 23, 2016 7:31 PM EDT

This is an excellent comment, B.

Thanks. I would say that most of the fighters I have dealt with have been ruined by such things as Joe hazarded here.

Big, Sweaty Bitches

The Confrontation Escalation Guide for the Real Black Man

Most of the men I write for are of the pale faced variety. I doubt if there's more than ten black fellas that read my site. But, half of the fellas that I coach are melanin-rich individuals, and they have a specific escalation danger. Most white guys have to worry about predation in vastly greater proportions than confrontation. On the other hand, athletic, young black men, while being at just as high a risk of predatory attack as his white counterpart, he is many times more likely to be challenged to a fight than a white man. This challenge will come from another black man.

This other black man will be carrying emasculation baggage so heavy, that he can't be helped. He will eventually be killed by one of his own or taken out by law enforcement. In the meantime, he will constantly lash out at confident black guys who have their act together. He won't pick on the nerds or the geeks, because there's no status to be gained. This man has always suffered severe, emasculating child abuse at the hands of his mother and is literally trying to build a masculine self-image at the expense of others. In behavioral terms, this guy is a bitch, because he was bitch raised. This does not necessarily mean that he's not a threat. He could be a very dangerous person.

The goals of the big, sweaty bitch build on one another. He feeds off of each, getting more emotional nourishment with each escalation.

Goal #1 is to punk you out, to get you to back down. This is basic primate posture and submit behavior. It's what is seen among gorilla males, as opposed to chimpanzees who are more murderous.

Goal #2 is to beat you down. If he can get you to behave accordingly, then any physical success he has by making you submit in a physical confrontation will pump him up more than simply punking you out. The guy that's aiming for this is primarily a legal danger to you. As soon as you turn the tables on him and beat him down, his litigious, bitch-raised upbringing will kick in, and he'll take legal action.

Goal #3 is to stomp you out or stab you. This is often a group goal with the big, sweaty bitch acting as the flash point for a mob attack on you. It is important for you to be able to decide if the surrounding people are observers waiting to see this guy try to implement #1 or #2, or if they are with him. If they are with him, then you're in a lethal situation.

Below are the verbal cues used by the big, sweaty bitch to get you to "act black." In many workplace and social settings, emasculated black men will go after a real black man who has his act together on an emotional level, trying to get him to act out in a way that will embarrass him in front of the larger society, a white boss, for instance. In a non-work place situation, he's working to compromise you in the eyes of the police. This system is hundreds of years old in the United States. It is a way in which people discontented by their social status but unwilling to advance drag those inclined to advance back down, like crabs in a basket do if one tries to climb out. This system of invalidation is based on verbal cues listed below with the correlating meaning, from least to most offensive.

1. Nigga is a term that means you are no better than I am and can have friendly and unfriendly applications; as soon as it is uttered, determine where it is going and act before it gets there.

2. My Nigga is a term of endearment that indicates that this person either wants your guard down, because you're about the be the subject of a predatory attack, or he really has no bad intentions and wants to make that clear. There's a lot of play here.

3. Nigger is a term designed to offend and place you beneath the offender. This is assault, plain and simple. The person saying this obviously wants you to attack him and also deserves to be attacked. If you can find a way to measure him out and then put him down, that's fine, but don't verbally escalate—don't say a damned thing.

4. Bitch is a blatant insult that declares you not to be a man if you do not engage in confrontation. You can usually walk away from this. If you don't want to walk away, I suggest you act like a bitch, but quietly, seeming to submit with your body language and then hitting him in the jaw while he runs his mouth.

5. Bitch-Ass Nigga is equivalent to bitch, act accordingly. This guy's just more articulate.

6. Bitch Nigger indicates that this dude really wants to fight or is utterly convinced that you're going to back down. How you handle this is really dependent on the situation. If this is a stomp out situation, you need to act decisively when this term comes out. This has often been used as a group attack cue.

7. Niggar is used by some black men when they are so enraged and have so much hatred for the person they are addressing that they are having difficulty not attacking. They are one the verge of an adrenaline dump. If you can avoid verbal engagement and physical contact for two minutes after this word is used, they'll melt down.

Little Debbie's Big Idea

Dealing with Little Dindu Bitches or Dindettes

I stopped at the Ghetto Mart for coconut water today and saw a sight.

Little Debbie is a big chick of Swedish descent who works as a cashier at a ghetto supermarket in Harm City, Maryland. She noticed that the lady who she had just checked out—a small, Dindu bitch in cut off jeans, wife beater and flip-flops with her hair woven with fake braids—had a box of fried chicken hidden under her shopping cart. She pointed to the security guard, who stopped the woman and asked her to pay for the chicken.

The little, 18-year-old-looking Dindette then began screaming, and swearing at Debbie, told her she wanted a refund, that it was Debbie's fault for not seeing the chicken, and that she was "from Wess Balmore, bitch," en we can take dis shit outside, where I'll whoop yo white ass—bitch!"

Debbie stepped out from behind the register and said, "Let's go, Bitch. I'll grab that wiglett of yours and scrub the sidewalk with your face!"

The Dindette, looking up at the husky paleface broad, then seemed to think better of her challenge, set the box of unpaid chicken on the register back, and left, looking over her shoulder nervously.

I love shopping at the Ghetto Mart.

Big, Hairy Bitches

The How and Why of the Postmodern Anti-Father

I was recently introduced to a sissy young man, who seemed tall, fit and full of potential, but could not look me in the eyes and shrank from shaking my hand. His relative, who had introduced us, then confided in me that he yelled at and scolded his daughter regularly—that the girl was withdrawing, losing her confidence, becoming "beaten down."

This was absolutely no surprise to me. In my mind, our horrific history of child abuse in this nation stems from this factor, emasculation.

The emasculated adult male is either a sissy pushover or a sissy bitch. Neither type of parent is effective at helping a young person form the type of resilient mindset necessary to take on our sick, soul-crushing world. The United States grew from a plantation economy that was entirely based on kidnapping, selling, working, beating and killing orphans and unwanted children from England, Ireland, Scotland and Africa, in that order. For the most part the only Americans who still savagely beat their children today are African Americans, who, with the encouragement of the political machine, have not managed to advance their culture beyond its 1868 Reconstruction form.

Therefore, black American males emerge into the world at a catastrophic emasculation rate, due largely to the savage bitches that raise them without a man.

However, white America is nearly as poorly served by the 40-year media and academic campaign to portray white men as sissies who come in two varieties, fools and fiends. There is the other, taboo media depiction of the white man—the psychopathic warrior, who is utterly incompatible with our society. But everything our children are taught drives them in the other direction with no chance to stop halfway and maintain societal approval. Where the savage black wench emasculates her boy with punches and kicks and crude insults, the postmodern American man either emasculates via pathetic example or invalidating reproach, and such invalidating reproach is also the perfect tool for crushing the spirit of a daughter, to guarantee that she will rebel and flee to the arms of some neutered savage upon coming of age; for the girl that is invalidated by the father seeks his opposite in type, but his inferior in will.

I commented to the person that introduced me to this bearded sissy that I had never known any of the many fathers I had trained with—who were, of course, fighters—to be cruel to their children. This is the salient family-building lesson one learns in the gym, whether on a boxing, MMA or stick-fighting team, that negative words have an insidious effect on the striving young spirit and wax more psychologically corrosive the closer the evil-speaker is to the target of his passive-aggression. Among fighters, negative reflections are usually couched in humor or in comparative analysis directed toward self improvement. To see a boxer with his daughter has always been a portrait of gentle strength, on his part when he's strong and on her part when he's nearly gone.

This sissy world of faceless man-things afraid of their own chest hair and composed of the type of invalidating mental life expressed in the comment sections of most of the websites I visit, is a strange field to me. It is also notable that the more positive tone on my combat-oriented site is reflective of the fact that large numbers of fighters frequent it, people to whom verbal sniping is counterintuitive and often degrading.

A woman who is merely a bitch still has a place at the human table, albeit a lowly one. But a man who is merely a bitch, or even more bitch than not, deserves to be knelt down behind an empty factory to join the rust of a more manly age in staining a land now lost to our lesser half.

Nice Bitches

A Serendipitous Triple Counterpoint to the Rampant Brutality of the Ebony Maternal

If you have read the last chapter of On Bitches you can see that the book was poised to finish on a low note. Then a trip to a large supermarket in a mixed race suburb to procure meal ingredients for my youngest son, placed me at a faithful intersection of maternal wills.

Charles had just beaten my ass out in the sun for about an hour and I was still mildly concussed from last week's whopping and reeling from the 100 degree heat of our stick-thwacking tryst. Presumably this and my lax shopping style rendered me into a sympathetic looking white daddy figure. As an obviously working class white man, I can tell you that no white woman of any social class or in any employment position in a grocery store, has ever done me the slightest kindness. Most will sneer or object if I hold the door, scurry away if I say excuse me, reach for their smart pone if I suggest helping them lift a heavy object. The only exceptions have been available single cashiers, who immediately upon seeing I wear no wedding ring, begin angling for a date with the next target of their soulless quest for material goods and viable dick strokes. In short, most white women I have had contact with in my life are nothing but decorated meat with enough brains to seek a high-earning meat-tickler. I consequently rate few white woman as human.

On the other hand, black woman, for the most part, are either callous imitations of these soulless white women or barbaric caricatures of some pre-human cannibal queen. Still though, although most black women are soulless beasts, I have more often met good women among their kind. [I have had little contact with Asian and Latina women, though the impressions are more positive than the black or white vagina pools.] My theory for this is that our society is designed to cultivate the worst kind of gold-digging, soul-eating white whore possible and that, so calibrated, it fails but rarely to produce this noxious creature. On the other hand, the inability of many black women to meet the national, Caucasian-based, beauty standard tends to bring out the best in few even as it guarantees the worst in most. Below is one of the many proofs of this I have encountered, as if God were reminding me that my recent experiences with the negative were not truly representative.

I was behind a 60-year-old woman with her own curled hair, wearing a tasteful summer dress and shopping with coupons.

Behind me was a 50-year-old woman, with her own hair, cut short, and wearing a tasteful blouse and shorts outfit with sandals.

The cashier was a young, model-pretty mulattress who weighed in at about 100 pounds and, like the two ladies to either side of me, spoke English and smiled naturally.

I was kind of out of it and was not used to shopping at these upscale suburban joints with the club card and the coupons and the stipulations attached to their use. Seeing the incompetently selected nature of my purchase, once on the belt, the lady ahead of me asked me a few questions and determined I didn't know what the hell I was doing and was going to end up spending 50% more than I should. They all pitched in with coupons and cards and advice for future shopping experiences with this store, and got me through the line paying $16 and change instead of $23 and change.

The final act consisted of the little cashier babe—who looks like the actress that plays the brothel madam on Black Sails, but lacks the French accent—not placing my change in my hand until she supported my receiving hand with hers. I must admit, in a hurry to my son's, I was having some tremors from not hydrating well enough after the training session and she apparently noticed this and didn't want me dropping my change. There was a genuine human tenderness to this encounter which elevated me from my haze as I walked back out into the sun...past two towering, scowling, whore-dressed ghetto bitches swearing like sailors about some dude they were about to "fuck up!"

In the future, when passing such savage wenches on the day-to-day, I will try to recall those two soft little hands making sure my swollen paw received its deposit while the lady behind encouraged, "There you go, sir. May you have a blessed day—and remember your discount card, okay."

» Add a comment «

Sam J.   July 28, 2016 8:30 PM EDT

If you've read any of comments you know I have no love for Blacks but Black Women can often be very sweet. I try to treat everyone I meet with civility no matter what color. White Women usually don't catch this but Black girls do frequently and feed it back.

Nero The Pict   July 26, 2016 9:21 AM EDT

James,

Thanks for publishing this piece. Your

observations about the racial divide among women are similar to my own in this regard. How much of the observed pattern that you speak of vis-a-vis the dichotomy between white women and black women do you think is geographic (aka a Baltimore thang') in nature???

I think I met the last white women still in possession of her soul in Baltimore about eight years ago. Alas, she was a Pictish transplant that had absconded south of Yo' Hadrians wall. Maybe that doesn't count.

In my early days I kept as my concubine a facsimile of the mulatress cashier you spoke of. I have many fond memories. She was one of the few among the many that I laid with who did not have a soul possessed by mercantile interests or pure vanity.

The older Black women that you speak of...do you think that in some ways they are like the older Black gentlemen at the mixed race sports bar? Preserving what is at this point (especially in that area) the dwindling arts of empathy hospitality and kindness that those females of our pale cast used to exhibit?

Living in the Northern lands as I do today...I can see the same scene that you describe being played out among the various tribes of women that inhabit this area. In the Baltimore hive, the only women that would likely come to your aid in such a fashion that were not black would probably be 80-year-old white ladies in Dundalk. Maybe.

JL responds: July 26, 2016 10:58 PM EDT

Glad you liked it, Nero.

For working class scrubs like us in Baltimore, the last vestiges of gentility are older black folks. The old white folks—like the Dundalk broads you spoke of—are usually tough and hard.

What I think this goes back to is slavery: The Irish were in the fields and the blacks were in the house, so they inherited the affectations of civility and if you make anything a habit it will change you along its lines...

Cold-Hearted Bitches

An Afterword to On Bitches: The Final Word on the Feminine Turd

Our society—in the West—elevated the woman above the slave girl of the East and accrued numerous benefits from this. For instance, our women became such demanding creatures, that, like the Iroquois warrior, or the Zulu impi man, driven forth beyond the cozy confines of the home to strive for female approval our ancestors won many a war against lesser men who had an obedient woman at home to kiss his slippered feet and a slave man to fight for him until the going got to tough and he got gone. We even had a number of queens who waged record wars, sending murderous men to the far corners of the globe to do their shrill bidding.

I will cover this entire complex in A Dread Grace, the nonfiction focus of the coming winter. Until then, as we are who we are where we are with what women have become, we should remember that the demanding wife only deserves her place on her pedestal when she has got our back, not when plunging a knife into it. In its bid to separate the uniquely complimentary gender team of the West, our advocate-masters for a global anthill society have all but torn us away from our women. There are a few reasons why:

1. When women have to work outside the home they develop resentment toward the man, though they will not admit this. When alone, with the state raising her children, this woman resents all men.

2. When men become weak from dependence on proxy aggression—when you no longer feel it is your duty to knock Tyrone's teeth down his throat for demanding your wallet, but believe that a uniformed officer of the state should do it for you—then you no longer illicit the yearning respect of your woman, though she

will never admit this. There is a reason why fighters—even old, never-was, potbellied Santa Clause hopefuls—attract women out of all proportion to their form, social status and earnings, and it is because, on a chemical level, they yearn for a hard man. Society has seduced American men into trying to be like women to gain female approval.

3. Entitlement is the oldest of the evils that separate people into aggressor and target. In the case of violence in society, I have found, and believe I have proved in 40,000 Years from Home, that a sense of entitlement is the number one indicator of aggressive behavior. This explains current black on white mob violence and former white on black mob violence in America. It also explains the following:

Two Beating Hearts

I am old enough now to have known many strong men whose hearts have failed them. I have two older friends from the martial arts community who have faced heart problems. Both of them were too proud to give me a head's up, just went to the hospital with the person that they had been conditioned by society to believe would take care of them in such a weakened state: their women. One was a wife the other a longtime, live-in girlfriend. These are both tough-bodied, tough-minded men, both having survived shootings, one in Vietnam the other in East Baltimore. But when the heart starts to go the will ebbs…

Mason was recovering from a heart problem related to severe dehydration. He could not relate all of the details as his wife had handled the paperwork and spoken to the doctors while he was unconscious and she took it all, on the day of his discharge. While he was waiting to be wheeled out the door on a hot August day, ten miles from home and eight miles from the karate studio, she took his records, his wallet, his phone, his bank card—which had just been infused with his monthly SSI—and the truck, and drove to Western Maryland to live with her sister. Standing alone in the heat he saw two choices, walk to the school, where I was training, or walk home. He walked into the school, took a long time getting ready, walked out onto the matt to applause and then confided in me he needed some help. My son and I bought his meals and arranged for his transport until his next check came...

Winston's heart was racing uncontrollably and he was admitted to the hospital. Still unable to stabilize his heart, the staff did permit his girlfriend's request to sleep in the chair in his room. As soon as the nurses were gone she began demanding his bank card, saying that she had a date with another guy and that guy was broke and she needed to eat. Suddenly aware, that this cruel bitch had merely been using him for years and that she didn't even have enough compassion to lift his card after he expired and go spend his money, but wished to discard him as he lay ailing, he said no to the woman he had always been so giving to. She then flew into a rage and was removed by security as she ranted and raved about her needs, what she deserved, what she was entitled to.

So young men, many old men before you have made the mistake of assuming reciprocal care, and of expecting the women they love to behave with honor, and have paid terribly in their final hours. We must understand that our society has done everything in its prodigious power to turn our women against us, to convince our women that we are a mere asset that they must manage and discard in accordance with the wishes of the vast social organism that they are merely an ingestion port of. The materialistic woman whose place on her pedestal is now held up by the State, rather than her man's earned admiration is the enemy of Mankind and of your very soul.

Test her for senses of entitlement and discard her when they are detected.

» Add a comment «

Sam J.   August 1, 2016 11:51 PM EDT

I have it in my mind that this is what happened to the Spartans. Their Women became entitled. They wouldn't have children, and they just wasted away.

What needs to be done is all Women's eggs should be removed and frozen when they are young. They don't have kids; guys should be able to buy them and implant them. There's a new genetic engineering technique called CRISPR. With it they can very specifically snip

DNA at a specific location and remove or add DNA. It's cheap and it will make gene engineering boom like you wouldn't believe. There will huge unbelievable changes in genetic engineering due to this. For example, if you added the immune system of a human to say, a cow, you could implant the embryo in the cow and have babies. Maybe it's not exactly easy but it could be done. I can't emphasize how important this CRISPR technique is going to be to biology. It's going to speed up to warp factor all genetic engineering. I think they're setting up the first human trials now. They're going to use it on cancer patients first. Probably because they're so close to dying. Eventually they're going to use it to snip out bad sections of DNA that cause disease. Say you have genes for sickle cell anemia. They could remove all the faulty genes that cause it. You could also use it to make your kid have blue eyes, be smarter, stronger... it gets fairly hairy.

https://en.wikipedia.org/wiki/CRISPR

http://time.com/4380352/crispr-human-trial-us/

B August 1, 2016 2:10 PM EDT

To keep women on the straight and narrow, you need a serious community with religious values, and preferably you need to be raising kids together.

'Snatched Her Punk-Ass'

Women Get Mauled and Killed by Tiger While Trying to Assault Husband at Zoo!

Unfortunately, a beautiful male lion was killed over mangling one of these stupid bitches.

I wonder what the Chinese would think of Tommy judging them?

I was going to throw a bitch-eating party, but thought better of it. Even so, this video is heartening—continental breakfast anyone?

Simba?

Muffasa?

Intwidemahu?

https://www.youtube.com/watch?v=fdozeHbVv9E

» Add a comment «
Jeremy Bentham August 7, 2016 11:19 PM EDT

Hey, no jokes about Chinese takeout now...that's not who we are.

Chinese women? Tony says they're GRRRR-EAT!

Sam J. August 4, 2016 10:49 AM EDT

This was really funny.

Eddie's Corner

A Paleface Crack Dealer Discusses Slinging Ready Rock in Dindustan

I can't stand bitches and it seems anymore that every young buck out there is a bitch, just like their mothers, talking shit with no balls to back it up. You'd think niggers were the masters of everything the way they talk. I was down in Saint Helena with my boy—not my usual spot, just meeting my boy on the corner, makin' sure he's good—when this skinny kid steps up, off a bike, and holds a nine on us, you know, ghetto sites, looking down the side of the Barretta—definitely a Barretta. He was maybe seventeen—fuckin' punk-ass bitch.

I said, 'What?' [shrugs shoulders]

Then I notice the bitch is froze up, like he's dead.

I step to him [crowds author, holding his own finger and thumb to represent a handgun, pressing the 'barrel' to his sternum], "Wha'?, Wha'? Bitch, bitch-you man enough ta pull it, use it."

This dude was froze solid, like a dude that's been dead all day. What a bitch! I mean I took nigger guns before and whipped their asses, but never this easy. He couldn' even talk, never said a word, just big eyes flaring open like he'd seen a ghost. Now, I'm checkin' on my boy, this is his corner. Came down to make sure he was good. This bitch—it turns out later when I talked to his people—he's a Turner Station boy—was just looking for people to rob. This wasn't no thing.

I stepped off and yanked the nine out of his hand and whipped his face a few times—maybe more than a few times. He just sat down and took it. Thing about dealing with bitches is you never know when they're going to bring in the pigs. I threw the gun down the storm drain. I already had two bitch-nigger nines en didn't need another. The bitch actually filed a complaint with his people—can you fuckin' believe that? That shit is disgraceful.

So I met them just outside of Turner Station to sort this shit out. Really, we're fucking slinging dope and you're going to file an excessive force complaint like I'm a fucking pig? Nigger, please! I told 'em I didn't mind them running bitches up my way, just that I wish they'd send some cuter ones and not expect me to let them point guns in my face.

Talking about bitches, I live across the street from this white faggot out in the County. I have plenty of property and popped off a few rounds over the water with the first nine I took. I kid you not, the pigs roll up in five minutes and that cocksucker is pointing at me where I'm sitting on the patio. I had cleaned up the brass and stowed the iron. The cop asks me if I'm shooting and I say, "Yeah, I got a paint ball, a pellet, and an airsoft—there a law against that, officer?"

I've been getting shaken down by the pigs since I was eleven. You just give em the 'I'm not your fucking boy' look, tell them what you want them to know, and what do they got? They fuckin' got nothin.'

Fuck 'em. I hate pigs and bitches but you have to be able to deal with them according to their ways. Mind you, I do not go breaking bad with a real bad motherfucker. I've met plenty of black dudes who were bad news and I treat them with respect. But those guys aren't goin' ta have any time [respect/breathing space] for you if you let the bitches pop off at the mouth or if you fold in front of the pigs.

It's a bitch world, brother.

I Didn't Expect a Hen House

Ex-Military Man Wonders How He Can Adjust to the Emasculated Law Enforcement Work Place

"James, I was so looking forward to being a cop, figured I would apply myself just like I did in the military, just like I did in the martial arts. I simply asked, 'What do I need to do to make it to the next level. What do I need to know and what tasks do I need to accomplish to make sergeant?'

"Even though I thought I was entering a man cave it turned out to be a hen house. I am actually working with bitches. My gung ho attitude, that's served me well in the military, has turned me into a pariah. Do you have any experience dealing with this kind of thing? And, most importantly, how do I accomplish this without impinging upon my own sense of honor, without knuckling under and playing their womanly games."

-Mavis

And I thought I was done writing On Bitches?

Well, with more bitches defecting from the masculine ranks every day than graduate from girldom, how can such a line of inquiry ever run dry?

It's good to hear from you Mavis. With the exception of sports, the military and certain trades—like construction, largely being taken over by Mexicans in my area—masculinity is always regarded as a threat by management and male coworkers. Law Enforcement and work in fire departments does come with military trappings and also dangerous tasks that lend an aura of masculinity. However, there is a huge difference between sports and military and police and fire.

In sports and the military most people are in for a decade or so as the meat that gets run through the grinder of character formation and masculine tempering. A tiny minority will remain as career instructors and aging grunts.

Conversely, in police and fire and other government jobs, people are signing up to get in on the early retirement feedbag. They're entire career is about the pension.

Comparing the mentality of the military man, athlete and entrepreneur to that of the employee, the cop the fireman and the retail outlet manger is like comparing the narrative needs of the horror fan with the romance reader.

My experience working as a staff member and manager in dozens of retails food operations, many of them unionized jobs where employees would do anything to hang on for the pension [most of these pensions have been raided or longtime union members ruthlessly culled by a Union-Management cabal]. I was headhunted from a private outfit to go into a union shop and work at a level above that which union workers regard themselves as being morally obligated not to fulfill. The bench mark was

200 cases per night and I could do 400. The new, larger markets needed people with private company work ethics and could not function with the minimal output union work ethic. This made myself and other acquisitions [UFCW Local 27 has since banned this practice and bars employers from starting outside talent off at top rate, causing one chain after another to lose ground against non-union outfits as they can no longer cherry pick the best non-union help.]

This situation made me hated based on productivity alone and the instinct was for me and the other outsiders to band together, which was facilitated by the fact that we were usually utilized in Frozen and Dairy, the two hardest sections. Eventually, the ostracism became hard for the other outsiders and they drifted back into the non-union workplace. But I stayed and eventually got into dry grocery—easy street!

I worked this by refusing promotion. I turned down nine promotions, until eventually the other guys saw me as their defacto shop steward. I cut my own deals outside of union channels with the store managers, even training assistant managers, and night captains and doing the technical work for my idiot grocery managers. Eventually, though they all hated me, they trusted me and became addicted to my helping hand. Despite universal hatred of me by labor and management [labor hating me for my high laboring output and management hating me for spurning their advances] I became everyone's go to guy, the guy that will do the shitty work, the guy that knows how the ordering machine works, the guy that will do the audit that my idiot assistant can't do, etc. It took 10 years of rocky road to earn five years of clear sailing.

Eventually after 15 years in the chains, a private outfit offered me the top spot. I went from bottom man on a night crew [although I was doing tasks assigned to grocery managers, night captains and assistant managers] to general manager in charge of 110 people. After 4 years doing better at that then men with 20 years management experience, I resigned and became the bottom man on a night crew in a private outfit and happily remain there, having proven that I have no ambition by my resignation. Below are the methods I developed for allying the fears of my coworkers.

1. Realize that most of your coworkers are idiots who see themselves as having no value outside of their current job track and will do almost anything to maintain their spot. A person with a tracking mentality will have extreme resentment for anyone who expresses an interest to advance ahead of them, so never inquire as to how one might advance—ever. Look for advancement in an outside organization. Be a cop in one city, amass an excellent record and apply for detective in another municipality, perhaps a higher-paying, lower-risk municipality than the one you cut your teeth in. If your coworkers believe that you have ambitions inside of their organization they will break out the knives. This static workplace was the final emasculating cut that began with agriculture. You might be a cop, armed like a warrior of an earlier time, but you work with males who are psychologically wounded women.

2. Your ambitious nature has been unveiled so demonstrate to your coworkers that you fulfill it elsewhere, in sports, or in a social

organization like a church. Once I began fighting again and making money coaching and writing and selling books—although it was mere change—my coworkers inflated it in their envious mind's eye and became less threatened by me in the workplace, knowing that I was directing my superior potential away from their job track and sometimes even hoping that if I took one of those promotions I turned down that I might take them along for the ride.

3. When you help a coworker never take credit but bestow credit on him. I do this all the time. Once they see that you are willing to let them take credit for your good work they will often protect you, wanting you around as you have become a crutch.

4. Learn from your coworkers by observation and then compliment them on their best skill. Train that skill until you are better than they are, all the time insisting that they are the best. Once this game wears thin and your boss says, "Hey, Mavis, you're the best cop we have for kicking in doors." Insist that you learned everything you know from the asshole that refused to properly instruct you because he

was jealous of his door-kicking ability. It is a Clintonian truth you might say, because you learned more from watching the idiot and correcting his flaws than he ever could have taught you.

5. Ask advice, even of those who hate you. If they give you bad advice hoping you screw up, simply thank them and fail to apply their suggestion. You will find some who will genuinely warm to you and others who will try and do you in for putting yourself at their mercy. Tactically—the workplace is a tactical environment from which you are extracting income in competition with others—you gain from this by not seeming as threatening and also by discovering who is after you and who is not, sooner rather than later.

6. Never mention your coworkers' shortcomings and be sure to mention their strengths, not as direct compliments, but by saying to a third employee, "Hey, Joe is really a great driver." Since you work with bitches you can expect them to gossip and pass this information around so it won't sound like you are sucking directly up to Joe.

7. Minimize your verbal output and maximize your physical output, which always, subconsciously gains you respect among men. However, it will draw some of the extreme bitches out after you as they have developed Masculinity Toxicity Syndrome or MTS, the pathological fear of real men by those who left their balls smoking on the altar of the Goddess.

8. If an extreme bitch is acting as your supervisor, then make it a game where you will crush them with your dedication. I do this with racist blacks who act hatefully toward me by being extremely kind and making them choke on their hate. At work I've done it by doing more and coming back for my next assignment sooner, wearing down my super's nerves by making him boss beyond his comfort zone.

9. Keep a journal. By writing down names, times and dates concerning your work performance you will be better prepared to face accusations by the downright evil coworker who will occasionally pop up and try to get you fired just because he can't stand being in proximity to a quality man. Being able to cite times, dates and details concerning your work record is

often all you need to refute later claims, because when people lie about coworkers they generally lie about something they—from the simian vantage of their sub-literate mind—believe to be too far in the past to be easily refuted.

10. Reward the pussies you work for and those you work with who do not go after you by doing them incidental favors without any ostentatious display. These bitches live in a pecking order, a female mind frame which measures many little slights and props that real men tend to overlook as they focus on their goals. Throw the bitch a bone: pick up his hat, buy him a coffee, cover his ass [as far as legally/ethically possible], wish him a good weekend, compliment him on a great effort, whatever it takes to convince him that you are not competing with him, because you cannot. Even if you are going head-to-head for the same position, men do not compete with women, so if he expresses an interest in the position you want, recommend him for it and support him. Come on, Marvis, if your wife and you were looking at hats and you only had enough money for one, you'd buy hers and wait for yours,

right? That is the true burden of a man, as well as the measure of his quality: that there are so many bitches and so little time to help them all feel good about themselves while you grin masculinely down.

Good luck, Marvis.

» Add a comment «
Sam J. August 15, 2016 9:43 PM EDT

"...Ask advice, even of those who hate you...."

It's known psychological ploy/trait/whatever that if someone helps you they will be more favorable to you because now they have something invested in you.

Might want to look at this. This guys writes books on influence. He's good. It's likely he recently started working with Hillary and that's why she's doing better. Here's a short pdf on the major points of his work.

http://www.influenceatwork.com/wp-content/uploads/2012/02/E_Brand_principles.

pdf

I know some of this stuff but don't really practice it because it's too deceitful for me, BUT it might at let you know what NOT to do. Don't negatively influence people. I have used it this way on occasion. However I'm mostly too hardheaded to kiss to people very well.

One thing bad about reading this book is you start to realize just how often people and the idiot box are using these techniques to brainwash you into doing something they want. It becomes very annoying when you see them deliberately doing this.

Ismael   August 14, 2016 5:57 PM EDT

James, thank you, damn you da man, I will print this and hand out upon my retirement, have practiced some of the methods above, but you have taken it to a whole new level!

There is No End to Bitches

www.ingramcontent.com/pod-product-compliance
Lightning Source LLC
Chambersburg PA
CBHW060234290526
45789CB00001B/45
* 9 7 8 1 5 3 7 3 7 4 0 0 0 *